THIS PRESENT REALITY

Breaking the Timeline of our Adversary

UNDERSTANDING THE SPIRITUAL
DYNAMICS OF OUR TIME

MADSON BAPTISTE

Copyright © 2019 Madson Baptiste.

All rights reserved. No part of this book may be used or reproduced by any means, graphic, electronic, or mechanical, including photocopying, recording, taping or by any information storage retrieval system without the written permission of the author except in the case of brief quotations embodied in critical articles and reviews.

This book is a work of non-fiction. Unless otherwise noted, the author and the publisher make no explicit guarantees as to the accuracy of the information contained in this book and in some cases, names of people and places have been altered to protect their privacy.

WestBow Press books may be ordered through booksellers or by contacting:

WestBow Press
A Division of Thomas Nelson & Zondervan
1663 Liberty Drive
Bloomington, IN 47403
www.westbowpress.com
1 (866) 928-1240

Because of the dynamic nature of the Internet, any web addresses or links contained in this book may have changed since publication and may no longer be valid. The views expressed in this work are solely those of the author and do not necessarily reflect the views of the publisher, and the publisher hereby disclaims any responsibility for them.

Any people depicted in stock imagery provided by Getty Images are models, and such images are being used for illustrative purposes only. Certain stock imagery © Getty Images.

Unless otherwise indicated, all Scripture is taken from the King James Version of the Bible.

Scripture quotations taken from the New American Standard Bible® (NASB), Copyright © 1960, 1962, 1963, 1968, 1971, 1972, 1973, 1975, 1977, 1995 by The Lockman Foundation Used by permission. www.Lockman.org

Scripture taken from the New King James Version®. Copyright © 1982 by Thomas Nelson. Used by permission. All rights reserved.

ISBN: 978-1-9736-7962-2 (sc)
ISBN: 978-1-9736-7963-9 (hc)
ISBN: 978-1-9736-7961-5 (e)

Library of Congress Control Number: 2019918082

Print information available on the last page.

WestBow Press rev. date: 11/13/2019

Contents

Introduction vii
Preface ix
Acknowledgments xi

Exposing the Kingdom of Darkness 1
The Three Cultural Realms 6
The Meaning of Life—Heirs of God 21
The Human Condition—Driven by Our Adamic Nature 26
Understanding Monotheistic Religions 30
The Spiritual Dynamics of the Soul 36
Those Who Are Perishing 39
The Time of the Removal of Restraint 47
Principalities and Powers 62
Rulers of Darkness 72
Spiritual Wickedness in High Places 74
The Enemy Within 81
This Present Reality 98

To the Believers in the United States 119
About the Author 125

Introduction

WE ARE LIVING IN a day when, for our destiny of redemption to be secure, we must do a critical evaluation of the world and our place in it. A season of great change is upon the earth, and the ability of this generation's church to navigate successfully through it is of the utmost importance if we are to stay on task to complete the great commission and fulfill our own personal destinies. During these times of change where God is moving His people through differing seasons toward accomplishing His purposes, many have lost focus, and lack understanding of what is required to move forward in their journey and to ultimately come to a place of completion. Unfortunately, moving from glory to glory is not as easy as we would like it to be. Many churches have adopted antiquated, illegitimate, and/or immature postures, finding themselves losing ground when dealing with the frustrations of an ever-changing spiritual climate. The church is, it would appear, like Joshua which in his day found itself wandering aimlessly, not understanding how to complete its assignment of establishing the kingdom of God in the earth. The growing globalization movement is a clear sign of the adversary's aligning the governments of this world against the government of God and the establishment of God's kingdom of righteousness. This is hallmarked by the accompanying removal of restraint we are witnessing: as cultural boundaries that historically have been the guideline by which the nations have been led are seemingly dissolving, and the church is now being called to a higher level of expectation, being forced to deal with issues that have been mostly avoided in previous generations. The chapters of *This Present Reality* are a series of letters and teachings written to a pastor in Pakistan who reached out for guidance as resources there are limited. My hope in sharing them is to assist you in understanding the current spiritual climate in the season we are experiencing, hopefully giving you the knowledge and wisdom to shift into a more authentic expression of your faith as our generation navigates this season of God's timeline.

Blessings. Madson Baptiste

Preface

REGARDLESS IF YOU'RE A new believer or if you have been in the faith for years, if you're struggling to find wisdom to overcome adversity in your life, these letters are written for you. Throughout the ages, the church has taken on various forms of expression and direction, but today more than ever Christian needs clarity and guidance to navigate through this ever-changing spiritual climate and to understand the often-confusing mix of information and misinformation found in various church, media, and internet resources. Some churches are embracing ungodliness in an effort to stay culturally relevant; services have become rhetorical, and church activity has been internalized, making programs and activities in the church more like community centers that cater to the desires of the flesh more than they serve the purposes of God. Equipping the saints for the work of ministry, conforming to the image of Christ, and bringing the church to unity of the faith have become forgotten goals to the once thriving and overcoming people of God. In the following pages, we will examine the current revelation of the global cultural shifts taking place in light of scripture. My hope is that these writings will facilitate breakthroughs for you and give you the freedom to serve God acceptably and passionately with boldness and without fear.

Acknowledgments

THERE ARE A FEW select people the Lord used to assist in my transition from a mediocre expression of faith, both in my personal and professional life. I would like to thank first the Lord Jesus Christ, who chose me long before I chose Him, and my wife and our three children, who supported me through the seasons of trial and change we suffered through. Finally, my mother Gene Wood who prayed for me to be a man of God from my youth.

My spiritual mentors, Apostles Thamo Naidoo, N. J. Varughese, Sam Soleyn, Dr. Sagie Govender and Dr Ed Smith. My spiritual brothers Carlo Griseta, Elbert Parker, Hayden Groves and Pastor David Frech who walked me through years of frustration with their wisdom and, by their example, helped me develop a compassion for those who serve the body of Christ. And even though we have never met in person Ravi Zacharias of RZIM ministries. Special thanks to Apostle, Randolph Barnwell in Durban S. Africa and Prophet, Shaun Blignaut in Port Elisabeth S. Africa. I am privileged to know you.

Scripture quotations marked "KJV" are taken from the King James Version of the Bible.

Unless otherwise noted scripture, references are taken from the King James Version of the Bible.

Scripture quotations designated (*NASB*) are taken from the *New American Standard Bible*. Copyright © 1960, 1962, 1963, 1968, 1971, 1972, 1973, 1975, 1977 by The Lockman Foundation. Used by permission.

Scripture quotations marked "NKJV" are taken from the New King James Version. Copyright © 1982 by Thomas Nelson, Inc. Used by permission. All rights reserved.

THE CONTENT OF THESE LETTERS WERE
EDITED FOR THE BOOK VERSION.

Exposing the Kingdom of Darkness

TO THE CHURCH IN Pakistan and to my friend and brother in ministry Pastor Tariq, greetings from the church here in the USA and from all the saints who are keeping you in prayer. I thank the Lord for the good reports we see in your social media posts of the work you're doing in Pakistan. We are all encouraged, by hearing of your faith and good works, which are an example to many. Because of the difficulties of traveling to you and the sense of expediency that I have toward you, it seemed good to me that I should write to you concerning those things that are coming upon the earth, seeing as I was present when the first wave of the Holy Spirit came announcing the apostolic season, since its inception in the late 1980s. We now know that we are in the day when the fullness of the knowledge of God is being revealed. Even so, not everyone has received in themselves the understanding of the mystery of God that is unfolding. Therefore, do not be overly concerned about these things that are

> The Lord is intervening in the affairs of men and breaking the timeline of the adversary and the Globalist movement.

happening around the world. Everything is as it should be. The Lord is intervening in the affairs of men and breaking the timeline of the adversary and the Globalist movement. Just as the apostle Paul wrote in 2 Thessalonians 2, about a day that would come when there would be a great falling away, when lawlessness would abound, and the removal of the one who restraint would come so that those who are perishing will believe the lies and unrighteousness that have consumed the entire world. These people believe not the truth so that they may be saved but are being deceived. That day that Paul described has most assuredly come upon us.[1] Therefore, do not be ignorant of the times and seasons, but have wisdom and understanding of the knowledge of the days that are ahead. Many of the current publications I've read, have focused on the earthly issues of our day. Having a more thorough understanding of these things, I thought it more beneficial for you that our attention be on the heavenly activity of which Paul also wrote: "We battle not against flesh and blood but against principalities, power, rulers of darkness, and spiritual wickedness in high places."[2] These celestial beings,

---

[1] 2 Thessalonians 2:5–7, 11–12: "Do you not remember that while I was still with you, I was telling you these things? And you know what restrains him now, so that in his time he will be revealed. For the mystery of lawlessness is already at work; only he who now restrains will do so until he is taken out of the way. … And for this cause God shall send them strong delusion, that they should believe a lie: That they all might be damned who believed not the truth but had pleasure in unrighteousness" (NASB).

[2] The following are definitions of words and phrases appearing in Ephesians 6 as found in James Strong, *Strong's Expanded Exhaustive Concordance of the Bible* (Nashville: Thomas Nelson, 2009):

Principalities—arche (ar-khay'): the first place, principality, rule, magistracy; used of angels and demons.

Powers—exousia (ex-oo-see'-ah): the power of rule or government (the power of him whose will and commands must be submitted to by others and obeyed).

Rulers of darkness—kosmokrator (kos-mok-fat'-ore); skotos (skot'-os): (1) a world ruler, an epithet of Satan: a lord of the world, prince of this age, the Devil and his demons; (2) used of ignorance respecting divine things and human duties, and the accompanying ungodliness and immorality.

which from the beginning were created to serve, now dwell among us in a heavenly dimension of darkness[3] having been cast out of God's presence. They are now always at work, attempting to gain control over us to fulfill the agenda of our adversary (Satan). Remember—when I first spoke to you about this, I explained that because of the free will of mankind, God has established the corporeal principle in that celestial deities, because they exist in other realms, must have human instrumentation to carry out their will on the earth. And the bridge between the spiritual realm and our own realm is the consciousness of human beings and our ability for introspection with the free will and the consequences that come from the temptations of, the lust of our eyes, the lust of the flesh, and the pride of life.[4] God is always looking for someone to intercede or "stand in the gap" on His behalf. However, because of boundaries of free will and choice, both are limited as to what can be accomplished by anyone who is submitting themselves to these spiritual influences. It is the order of

---

Spiritual—pneumatikos-(pnyoo-mat-ik-os'): belonging to a spirit, or a being higher than man but inferior to God.

Wickedness—poneria (pon-ay-ree'-ah): (1) depravity, iniquity, wickedness, malice, evil purposes, and desires; (2) persons in whom darkness becomes visible and holds sway.

High places—epouranios (ep-oo-ran'-ee-os): used of darkened eyesight or blindness, physical and mental power, the ability or strength with which one is endowed, which he either possesses or exercises.

[3] Job 18:7–8, 15–21: "The steps of his strength shall be straightened, and his own counsel shall cast him down. For he is cast into a net by his own feet, and he walketh upon a snare. ... It shall dwell in his tabernacle, because it is none of his: brimstone shall be scattered upon his habitation. His roots shall be dried up beneath, and above shall his branch be cut off. His remembrance shall perish from the earth, and he shall have no name in the street. **He shall be driven from light into darkness, and chased out of the world. He shall neither have son nor nephew among his people, nor any remaining in his dwellings. They that come after him shall be astonied at his day, as they that went before were affrighted. Surely such are the dwellings of the wicked, and this is the place of him that knoweth not God"** (KJV, emphasis added).

[4] 1 John 2:16: "For all that is in the world, the lust of the flesh, and the lust of the eyes, and the pride of life, is not of the Father, but is of the world."

creation in the world, seeing that God has given the earth to mankind to possess it but has also given Satan, as a prince, power over it using his Babylonian system, which will eventually be overcome by the church. Our example of conquering this system of control is found in Israel's possessing of the land of Canaan. It is the worldly system that is to be replaced by the people of God and His kingdom of righteousness. The Israelites would eventually accomplish this under the rule of King David HaMelech[5] the son of Jesse[6] from the tribe of Judah. The scriptures declare that God's enemies were defeated on every side and that the land had rest.[7] In the days of Joshua, the people of God were given the land across the Jordan River in Canaan to possess. It was a highly developed land of wealth and opportunity by a people who did not know God—a pagan land, but also a fruitful one. And it was God's desire that His heirs would be the recipients of a kingdom, only they were under the law, and therefore they were also under judgment.[8] Understand that being under the law brings judgment and is earthly, but in the new covenant, Christians are both earthly and heavenly, being under grace and receiving in themselves the Holy Spirit, which was not possible for them under the first covenant. The first covenant was given so that the benefits of the second in contrast would be revealed. It is a reflection given us so that

---

[5] The name HaMelech means "learned to be king."

[6] The name Jesse means "God exists" or "God's gift."

[7] 1 Chronicles 22:17–18: "David also commanded all the princes of Israel to help Solomon his son, saying, Is not the Lord your God with you? and hath he not given you rest on every side? for he hath given the inhabitants of the land into mine hand; and the land is subdued before the Lord, and before his people."

[8] Hebrews 12:26–29: "Whose voice then shook the earth: but now he hath promised, saying, yet once more I shake not the earth only, but also heaven. And this word, Yet once more, signifieth the removing of those things that are shaken, as of things that are made, that those things which cannot be shaken may remain. Wherefore we are receiving a kingdom which cannot be moved, let us have grace, whereby we may serve God acceptably with reverence and godly fear: For our God is a consuming fire."

we can clearly understand[9] and, by the example of the Israelites, learn from their mistakes and successes. Thereby we can willfully avoid the judgment they experienced under the law. Today the people of God do not displace others through violence but instead invite them to participate in the good news of the gospel of Jesus the Christ by His grace, whereby every kingdom of the earth will eventually come under the rule of the eternal kingdom of our God.[10]

Past generations have placed more emphasis on the earthly or terrestrial activity of the church and have believed that during this time of the removal of the one who restrains, the church must shift its attention away from its evangelical model and place more emphasis on engaging the heavenly activity that is at work as the global cultural shifts we are experiencing cannot successfully be challenged by an introverted, immature church. I think it necessary to expose the kingdom of darkness and its attributes so that the maturing church can more effectively address how to overcome and dismantle it.[11] Which in the light of the gospel of Jesus Christ, the church can accelerate its mission to restore mankind into the fellowship we had in the beginning with our heavenly Father. Therefore, we must understand that principalities, powers, rulers of darkness, and spiritual wickedness in high places make up the hierarchy of authority in the kingdom of darkness, and they operate from a platform of three distinct cultures, theonomous culture, heteronomous culture, and autonomous culture, which form the chessboard by which all celestial activity operates on the earth, and by which ever nation and government of men operate from.

---

[9] 1 Corinthians 10:11: "Now all these things happened to them for ensamples: and they are written for our admonition, upon whom the ends of the world are come."

[10] Revelation 11:15: "And the seventh angel sounded; and there were great voices in heaven, saying, the kingdoms of this world are become the kingdoms of our Lord, and of his Christ; and he shall reign for ever and ever."

[11] Matthew 16:18: "And I say also to thee, that thou art Peter, and upon this rock I will build my church: and the gates of hell shall not prevail against it."

The Three Cultural Realms

THEONOMOUS CULTURE IS THE ideology of societies that believe in intelligent design and natural law and that believe in a monotheistic or "one God" concept (e.g., Christians, Jews, and Muslims believe in one God), concluding that most attributes of life are self-evident (the way God designed them to be). The writers of scripture believed in natural law. Even though we are abandoning these beliefs in Western culture, it is foundational to the church and to God's kingdom culture that you recognize and reinforce these values among the believers under your care. Now each of these systems has pros and cons. The primary weaknesses of theonomous culture are the spirits of religion, unbelief, and idolatry.

Heteronomous culture is an ideology of elitist control and is contrary to the freedom found in Western cultures. A heteronomous

> Principalities, powers, rulers of darkness, and spiritual wickedness in high places—this is the hierarchy of authority in the kingdom of darkness, and these things operate from a chessboard of three distinct cultures: theonomous culture, heteronomous culture, and autonomous culture.

culture is one where the people are not self-ruled but are ruled by the minority elitist. There are many examples—communism, socialism, fascism, and Islam. Heteronomous leaders exercise extreme control over the people and, given that the majority of deaths and inhuman suffering have happened within such cultures, they are tyrannical in nature. This is the primary system our adversary uses to dominate mankind, and it will be the main example of our discourse in the following letters. The other systems also have humanistic (self-serving) elements found in them. They are often led by charismatic people and use substructures (i.e., powers, rulers of darkness) to control the masses. We are currently witnessing the exposure of elitist and autocratic people who are driving the globalist movement (which opposes everything that is of God and His kingdom of righteousness, or right living). The current expression of heteronomous culture is the post-modernist movement and is the direct consequence of the removal of the one who restrains. This shift in God's timeline involves a threefold cord of God's positioning of Christianity as it moves into the period of its greatest influence. The first phase is the removal of restraint. The second phase is the manifestation of the sons of God, and the third is the fulfillment of the scriptures speaking of the last days. It is recorded in Isaiah, Micah, and Ephesians that God's kingdom will sit upon all the other kingdoms that rule in the earth and that through the church the wisdom of God will finally convince the fallen angels of God's wisdom in His having chosen us over them. Eventually these earthly structures will fail as mankind's desire for peace and prosperity will be found in our willful submission to God's kingdom of righteousness and rule under Jesus Christ.

Islam is a false theonomous religion within a heteronomous culture. Muslims are told among other things, when to eat, fast, and pray, with extreme discipline exacted upon those who question or do not submit to such control. Islam is the spirit of Cain. It is a works-based religion that seeks preference over its counterparts, and when it sees that its brothers' offerings are preferred, then its response is to kill its brother. However, Judaism and Christianity are theonomous ideologies operating within autonomous cultures. Judaism is under the law, and Christianity is under grace, which is why Islamists are trying to destroy Israel and the United States, because their darkness is exposed by our freedoms. As they cannot escape the darkness without rejecting their culture, this is a difficult but not impossible task. The beauty of the gospel is that in Christ we are set free. This is a gift no one may attain except through Jesus and Him alone, and no power on earth can stop it because it is freely given and received in the soul of everyone who believes.

> And it shall come to pass in the last days, ***that the mountain of the Lord's house shall be established in the top of the mountains,*[12] *and shall be exalted above the hills; and all nations shall flow unto it. And many people shall go and say, Come ye, and let us go up to the mountain of the Lord, to the house of the God of Jacob; and he will teach us f his ways,*** and we will walk in his paths: for out of Zion shall go forth the law, and the word of the Lord from Jerusalem. And he shall judge among the nations and shall rebuke many people: and they shall beat their swords into plowshares, and their spears into pruninghooks: nation shall not lift up sword against nation, neither shall they learn war anymore. O house of Jacob, come ye, and let us walk in the light of the Lord. (Isaiah 2:2–5)
>
> But in the last days it shall come to pass, that the mountain of the house of the Lord shall be established in the top of the mountains, and it shall be exalted

---

[12] Mountains are earthly structures to which mankind submits itself. Examples of such structures are as follows: (1) governments, federal and civil, including both military and police to enforce the rule of law; (2) family; (3) entertainment, the arts, TV, and sports; (4) information, news, and journalism; (5) education and politics; (6) social structures, relationships, church, and social media; and (7) economics, commerce, business, science, and technology.

above the hills; and people shall flow unto it. And many nations shall come, and say, ***Come, and let us go up to the mountain of the Lord, and to the house of the God of Jacob; and he will teach us of his ways, and we will walk in his paths: for the law shall go forth of Zion, and the word of the Lord from Jerusalem. And he shall judge among many people, and rebuke strong nations afar off; and they shall beat their swords into plowshares, and their spears into pruninghooks: nation shall not lift up a sword against nation, neither shall they learn war anymore***. But they shall sit every man under his vine and under his fig tree; and none shall make them afraid: for the mouth of the Lord of hosts hath spoken it. For all people will walk everyone in the name of his god, and we will walk in the name of the Lord our God for ever and ever. (Micah 4:1–4)

And to make all men see what is the fellowship of the mystery, which from the beginning of the world hath been hid in God, who created all things by Jesus Christ: ***To the intent that now to the principalities and powers in heavenly places might be known by the church the manifold wisdom of God,*** According to the eternal purpose which he purposed in Christ Jesus our Lord. (Ephesians 3:9–11)

All wars are fought over cultural conflicts. Understand that communism, socialism, fascism, and other forms of government are based on heteronomous culture. Currently in the United States there is a shift toward this system as Americans are foolishly giving up their autonomous culture for more government control as they have raised a self-serving generation and do not value the extraordinary level of freedoms afforded them. All of this is driven by the orphan spirit of fatherlessness and a spirit of covetousness, which leads us to the third type of culture, autonomous culture.

Autonomous culture is found predominantly in Western society where each person dictates his or her own moral prerogatives and where the value of the individual is recognized over the collective. In other words, you can live however you want if you agree to follow the law of the land and you don't violate the autonomy of your fellow citizens. This freedom is the catalyst that has taken the United States, Israel, and those countries that have adopted "autonomous constitutional republics" to the forefront of advanced civilization on the earth. The autonomous culture is the closest to God's kingdom culture because it facilitates mankind's free will. Mutual autocracy, however, has its problems because democratic societies position themselves as neither theonomous (according to natural law) nor heteronomous (dictatorial), and once autonomous societies lose their moral anchor, a subculture of humanism emerges as the catalyst for change towards an entitlement/welfare-based society instead of the free market capitalist system. The current expression of this is recognized as the postmodernist movement under the banner of socialism. Therefore, understand that democracy has become the expression of covetousness.[13] These cultures are always competing for control over mankind,[14] resisting the advancement of God's kingdom culture. All wars are fought over these competing

> "Now all these things happened to them for ensamples: and they are written for our admonition, upon whom the ends of the world are come. Wherefore let him that thinketh he standeth take heed lest he fall"
> 1 Corinthians 10:11–12

---

[13] Exodus 20:17: "Thou shalt not covet thy neighbor's house, thou shalt not covet thy neighbor's wife, nor his manservant, nor his maidservant, nor his ox, nor his ass, nor any thing that is thy neighbor's."

[14] Psalms 2:1–5: "Why do the heathen rage, and the people imagine a vain thing? The kings of the earth set themselves, and the rulers take counsel together, against the Lord, and against his anointed, saying, Let us break their bands asunder, and cast away their cords from us. He that sitteth in the

cultures. For example, just over one hundred fifty years ago, the United States fought a Civil War to abolish slavery. Over three hundred sixty thousand white Union soldiers gave their lives for the cause of freedom of an oppressed black African population. The autonomous culture founded in the United States Constitution overcame the internal heteronomous subculture of slavery in the Southern states. Recently, Brother Fazal, you've experienced similar recognizable warfare in your region through what many referred to as the Arab Spring, where freedom-seeking people sought to dislodge the repressiveness of the heteronomous cultures of the Middle East for the freedom of autonomous Western culture in the form of democratic republics. (Again, both of these systems are fueled by the orphan mentality [Adamic nature] inherent in mankind and our deep desire to bond with our Creator as we were created as symbiotic beings, and not created to operate independently apart from Him.) This leads us to our next position, namely, powers (i.e., *exousia*).

Powers are, among other things, governmental systems of control that manage society for the principalities they represent. This is necessary to maintain order and an environment wherein mankind may willfully come into the knowledge of God and His redemptive plan amid the backdrop of any inferior system. Otherwise you will have anarchy, which again is representative of the possession of the land of Canaan. God did not have the Israelites start over in a barren place when they departed from Egypt, which they could have accomplished in their desert wanderings to establish themselves as the people of God. Rather they displaced an inferior culture and replaced it with a superior kingdom. This is all part of God's design to reveal His lordship over all things. This may seem harsh to some, that these people who seemingly did nothing wrong to deserve their fate and were expendable, but for us this is an example of the ramifications of being under the law and being a reflection of "a type and shadow of things to come" and of the overthrow of the

---

heavens shall laugh: The Lord shall have them in derision. Then shall he speak unto them in his wrath and vex them in his sore displeasure."

illegitimate/demonic structures that stand in the way of the redemptive plan of God. For God had redeemed Israel for His purpose, and that was to replace the preeminent culture of the day with His kingdom culture. The Canaanites were Baal worshippers, which facilitated the second act of God's people, which was to attack the gates of hell as represented by a people who served the spirit of the age. First in Egypt it was the god of Amon, and then in the wilderness, when they would not wholeheartedly engage God at Mount Sinai, they crafted a bull to worship and participated in unseemly behavior. Now Gods desire was to have them overthrow the same spirit here in the land of Canaan. God was able to deliver the Israelites from Egypt but delivering Egypt out of them was a more difficult challenge as now they were being asked to physically engage in the process, whereas before while escaping Egypt they were only witnesses to it. He had worked the slave mentality out of them in the wilderness, and now they had to become part of the process. (Remember, Tariq, you are part of the process in the territory where God has you.) Unfortunately, the church in our generation has to some degree lost its sense of purpose and holiness. This is something we must restore if we are to serve God acceptably. This season of the Israelites again was a type and shadow of the days we now live in where judgment was the result of sin. But in our day, grace, compassion, mercy, and the love of God through the new covenant is measurable as it reflects against the terms of the old covenant it replaced. We are progressing toward receiving the kingdom through the redemptive process of the removal of the things that can be shaken so that the unshaken kingdom[15] is all that remains

---

[15] Hebrews 12:23–29: "To the general assembly and church of the firstborn, which are written in heaven, and to God the Judge of all, and to the spirits of just men made perfect, And to Jesus the mediator of the new covenant, and to the blood of sprinkling, that speaketh better things than that of Abel. *See that ye refuse not him that speaketh. For if they escaped not who refused him that spoke on earth, much more shall not we escape, if we turn away from him that speaketh from heaven: Whose voice then shook the earth: but now he hath promised, saying, yet once more I shake not the earth only, but also heaven.* **And this word,**

on the earth. This constant battle for control begun by these demonic hierarchies and the systems they use is what keeps mankind in bondage and under the rule of our adversary. What we saw in the Arab Spring was, instead of a peaceful transition, was a spiritual battle between two opposing powers where freedom-seeking people sought the benefits of US autonomy as opposed to the heteronomous, Islamic system they served, and warfare ensued. Unlike the servant nature of God's kingdom, the demonic nature is always in competition with itself for preeminence among its ranks.

During this time of the removal of restraint whereby the majority of people desire unrestricted autonomy, which was ushered in by the introduction of smartphone technology, we are now seeing a global return of everyone doing what is right in their own eyes.[16] Which is evident in the establishment of the current Millennial culture. Understand that the global communication we've achieved is a modern-day reflection of the Tower of Babel. The restraint of media control has been taken away, and mankind's ability to build and have a common communication method has

> **Understand that the global communication we've achieved is a modern-day reflection of the Tower of Babel. The restraint of media control has been taken away, and mankind's ability to build and have a common communication method has brought us to the brink of reaching a heavenly status, a reality that linear beings are ill-equipped for**

---

yet once more, signifieth the removing of those things that are shaken, as of things that are made, that those things which cannot be shaken may remain. Wherefore we are receiving a kingdom which cannot be moved, let us have grace, whereby we may serve God acceptably with reverence and godly fear: For our God is a consuming fire" (emphasis added).

[16] Judges 17:6: "In those days there was no king in Israel, but every man did that which was right in his own eyes."

brought us to the brink of reaching a heavenly status,[17] a reality that linear beings are ill-equipped for, which have given technology companies significant influence over us. Since the fall of Adam, humans have not been able to function in a multidimensional state of timelessness. We currently exist in a three-dimensional existence where time, space, and matter coexist to form the physical universe.[18] This is called a continuum; neither of these three states can exist without the other two, if the three-dimensional state is to be maintained. Neither can anything from these separate realms individually manifest here. Only the Father Himself has such power, and when He came, He came in the form of Jesus Christ, not only so that we could see His humanity, but also so we could see that even He submits to His own Word.[19] Therefore, Jesus is the Word become flesh.

> The governing principles of creation are driving everything toward God's predetermined outcome in both the terrestrial and celestial realms, which are subjected to the free will of mankind. The sovereignty of God will ultimately prevail in a remnant who will worship Him in sprit and in truth.

Also understand that there are three levels of existence called the heavens. The word *heaven* in its basic form simply means those things that are above the earth.[20] The third or highest

---

[17] Genesis 11:6–10: "And the Lord said, Behold, the people is one, and they have all one language; and this they begin to do: and now nothing will be restrained from them, which they have imagined to do."

[18] Genesis 1:1: "In the beginning [time] God created the heaven [space] and the earth [matter]."

[19] Psalms 138:2: "I will worship toward thy holy temple and praise thy name for thy lovingkindness and for thy truth: for thou hast magnified thy word above all thy name."

[20] 2 Corinthians 12:2: "I knew a man in Christ above fourteen years ago (whether in the body, I cannot tell; or whether out of the body, I cannot tell:

heaven is where God's throne rests, and it is the one that came first. The next heaven is the realm of mankind in the physical universe, which the scriptures call the day and night,[21] which is a reference to time. The third or last heaven is called darkness. A place without light or the presence of God, it is the abode of the adversary. When Lucifer was cast out of God's presence in heaven and to the earthly realm, he was constrained from the light to the darkness.[22] Night and day in this context are not the same as the things we refer to as daytime and nighttime. The latter are two-dimensional realms that cannot create a three-dimensional continuum; therefore, they cannot exist in a material sense simultaneously. The scripture refers to this as the first day,[23] and it was created before the sun and moon, which were created on the fourth day. Therefore, when God created the physical universe, His second act was to divide it into two sub realms that could not interact with each other except through the frequency of the soul and/or the spirit, also referred to as your consciousness. The light has authority over the darkness, which is why when you simply resist the devil, he will flee. He has no choice because darkness does not understand the light, just as angels did not understand God's wisdom when he chose us over them, even though we are under them in the order of created things. (This is a principle He uses throughout scripture, always to choose "the least of these.") To be in darkness is literally to be in the absence of the presence and knowledge of God, which again has preeminence in the created universe. The terms *daytime* and *nighttime* are a reference to light in

---

God knoweth); such an one caught up to the third heaven."
[21] Genesis 1:5: "And God called the light Day, and the darkness he called Night. And the evening and the morning were the first day."
[22] Job 18:18–21: "He shall be driven from light into darkness and chased out of the world. He shall neither have son nor nephew among his people, nor any remaining in his dwellings. They that come after him shall be astounded at his day, as they that went before were affrighted. Surely such are the dwellings of the wicked, *and this is the place of him that knoweth not God*" (emphasis added).
[23] Genesis 1:5: "And God called the light Day, and the darkness he called Night. And the evening and the morning were the first day."

time and darkness in time, respectively, which the scriptures also refer to as morning and evening, a metaphor which again establishes light in time as preeminent over darkness. This allows celestial beings that live outside of time to interact with mortal human beings. They have the immortality we will also have once we are changed.[24]

Scientists are now discovering these realities along with dark matter.[25] Even though they have yet to find proof of dark matter, they know it exists because they see its effects. It's fascinating to watch that the more that is revealed through science, the more the reality of what we know to be biblical truth is established. Ultimately the love of God through His church[26] will prove the wisdom of God to the principalities and powers that have opposed Him since their fall. It is important to know that much of the early scripture is designed to reveal divine protocol so that as we move through time toward God's ultimate desire, we learn how to function amid creation principles so that we are not distracted from our purpose by those things that stand against the kingdom we are inheriting. Remember—many are deceived by the work of the adversary.

---

[24] 1 Corinthians 15:51–54: "Behold, I show you a mystery; We shall not all sleep, but we shall all be changed, In a moment, in the twinkling of an eye, at the last trump: for the trumpet shall sound, and the dead shall be raised incorruptible, and we shall be changed. For this corruptible must put on incorruption, and this mortal must put on immortality. So when this corruptible shall have put on incorruption, and this mortal shall have put on immortality, then shall be brought to pass the saying that is written, Death is swallowed up in victory."

[25] The laws of physics show that the principle materials of the universe that bind everything together do not contain enough mass for them to work. Therefore, science hypothesizes that there must be more substance that is not currently accounted for. Otherwise the universe would be an archaic place void of the order of the materials that bind it together.

[26] Ephesians 3:9–11: "And to make all men see what is the fellowship of the mystery, which from the beginning of the world hath been hid in God, who created all things by Jesus Christ: To the intent that now to the principalities and powers in heavenly places might be known by the church the manifold wisdom of God, According to the eternal purpose which he purposed in Christ Jesus our Lord."

As a spiritual leader in your community, Tariq, you must be able to relate these truths and trace everything back to the fundamental principles of creation found in scripture so that it becomes not only the anchor by which everything is established but also indeed the only foundation on which all truth rests. Since instant global communication has released mankind from the restraint of media control, this freedom has both good and adverse consequences. Every system by which human beings live must have both freedom and boundaries if it is to be sustainably functional; otherwise you have anarchy. Freedom of choice is inherent to mankind, but freedom of consequences is not. These two attributes are required to worship God in spirit and in truth, which the Lord desires in both the individual and the corporate sense. Therefore, you're seeing governments (i.e., powers/exousia) move toward systematic globalization in an effort to stop the advance of God's kingdom of righteousness. It is their response to the theonomous culture that governs mankind by willingly submitting to the righteous standard of God in scripture, which is driven by universal principles established at Creation. It is also why places like the United States and Israel are under constant assault. Again, you see these truths in the scriptures, as well as the pattern of rejection of God's rule, which can be seen in Exodus 20:18–19.[27] When the people rejected a relationship with God, He gave them rules by which to govern themselves. The Ten Commandments were the first foundational guidelines, or what we refer to as cardinal rules, these were designed to align with principles established at Creation to drive successful living. Ever since that rejection, human beings have tried to establish forms of government so as not to submit to the rule of God, which is in our Adamic nature[28] of self-preservation.

---

[27] Exodus 20:18–19: "And all the people saw the thundering's, and the lightnings, and the noise of the trumpet, and the mountain smoking: and when the people saw it, they removed, and stood afar off. And they said unto Moses, speak thou with us, and we will hear: but let not God speak with us, lest we die."

[28] Genesis 3:7–8: "And the eyes of them both were opened, and they knew that they were naked; and they sewed fig leaves together and made themselves

We see this with Samuel. He was God's prophet, and God was to be King with Samuel as His spokesperson, but He was rejected because the people desired a king like the peoples of other nations had.[29] They desired to live in sin and keep accountability on the king. It is the same problem we live with today. Believers want to be part of the kingdom yet live in unaccountable sin. This is why we have some religious systems with a two-tiered system of clergy and laity. We want the pastor to deal with God so we can live in the world and attend an assembly only to clear our conscience at a weekly service we call church, not understanding that we, not our Sunday assembly, are the church.

I find it interesting that the most successful governments to date is the theonomous culture established in the US and Israel. The peace and prosperity afforded Israel is overshadowed by the violence against it by the Islamist peoples who surround it. Here the nation of Islam stands in the place of Cain, the son of Adam. Jews and Christians stand in the place of Abel (Israel does so under the law, and Christians do so under grace). When the two brothers came to offer a sacrifice to the Lord, Cain came with an offering of works by which he sought approval for his self-efforts, and the other came with an offering of faith. Since Abel had nothing to give of himself, he instead gave God a return on the investment God had entrusted to him, for he was a shepherd. Abel did not own the sheep but only cared for them. They belonged to his father, Adam. Cain tried to give God a return on that, which God had cursed, because it was the work of Cain's self-efforts, which was rejected. It is not that the Lord rejects offerings from the ground, but He does reject an offering that is not an honest reflection of the one making it. Cain's error was that he tried to gain God's approval by way of his self-effort (which is a form of pride) and not by his character. Abel's offering was to give God a return on

---

aprons. And they heard the voice of the Lord God walking in the garden in the cool of the day: and Adam and his wife hid themselves from the presence of the Lord God amongst the trees of the garden."

[29] 1 Samuel 8:19: "Nevertheless the people refused to obey the voice of Samuel; and they said, Nay; but we will have a king over us."

His investment. (This acknowledges the godly relationship and the patriarchal protocol and is not performance based. You cannot give God anything material because He owns all things. You can only acknowledge what God has done for you by offering a return on the investment He has made in you. This is the basis of your salvation through Jesus's sacrifice.) Now the Lord took the opportunity to encourage Cain to change, saying that then his offering would be accepted. However, Cain's response was to kill his brother instead of making the change requested by God.

Of the three religions that claim Abraham as their founder and that serve the same God of Creation, the first (Judaism) sees God as the Creator to be worshipped by keeping the law, and the second (Christianity) worships God through faith in the Messiah, the Redeemer who will reestablish the relationship Adam had with God as his Father. The Jews also hope for the Messiah but have not yet accepted that He has already come, because they are bound by the law and have not understood the scriptures fully. Islam, the third, is not a religion but a system of control over the Muslim who sees himself as the heir of Ishmael, Abraham's firstborn. Muslims believe they have a right to dominate and conquer the world for God through works. They have not understood that Ishmael was the son of Abraham's disobedience. Instead they believe he was a victim and that therefore their cause is justified. This is a leftist philosophy we see in politics, which primarily is rebellion spawned from anger toward God. It is behavior of the orphan mind-set. These three systems of control identified in cultural form as influencing mankind with their substructures of man-made developed governments (i.e., powers), we recognize as the systems by which all forms of earthly governments are established. The purpose of the church in this regard is to spread its influence as God's ambassadors to willingly bring mankind under God's sovereign rule,[30] because even with

---

[30] Revelation 11:15: "And the seventh angel sounded; and there were great voices in heaven, saying, The kingdoms of this world are become the kingdoms of our Lord, and of his Christ; and he shall reign for ever and ever."

mankind's best intentions, because of sin, Jesus Christ is the only King who can rule in righteousness. I'll write more on this later, for now be blessed in your family, business, and ministry; greet everyone for me; and pray that the Lord will make a way for me to come see you soon.

Blessings, Madson

The Meaning of Life— Heirs of God

BROTHER TARIQ, I WAS blessed to finally have come and ministered among you. It was truly a humbling experience to see the progress you're making, even with so few resources. And it was clear that the seeds sown were well received by you and the leadership. I look forward to coming to see you again as I'm able. Since my visit, I felt impressed that I should expound on certain teachings, starting with the meaning of life as it relates to God's plan for mankind. Much of scripture cannot easily be understood without some explanation of what God's plan and purpose was when He set into motion everything that would ultimately bring to fruition all that He desired to accomplish when He created us and the natural universe.

Before the beginning there was God. Before He created anything, He purposed something in His heart and devised a plan that He hid in Himself, which the scriptures call a mystery.[31] God's desire was that He would have heirs or beneficiaries, someone to whom He could show the glory of who He is by His ability to love beyond measure. The first step in His plan was to create the heavenly realm

---

[31] Ephesians 3:3–5: "How that by revelation He made known to me the mystery (as I have briefly written already, by which, when you read, you may understand my knowledge in the mystery of Christ), which in other ages was not made known to the sons of men, as it has now been revealed by the Spirit to His holy apostles and prophets."

where His throne abides, the place of His reign. It is a timeless place where He would establish His rule and where all the angelic hosts would serve Him. In heaven, there were three archangels, Lucifer, Michael, and Gabriel, the chief of whom was Lucifer. He had the honor of leading the worship of God and was ordained as the most beautiful of all God's creation. God then created the physical universe, a place of time with its billions of galaxies, solar systems, and planets. Within one of these solar systems He made a planet called earth, where He created these little mud creatures that He called men. After this He informed the angelic hosts that their role was to serve mankind, that we would judge them, that we, not they, would become the beneficiaries of everything He had to give, and that they were created to serve and not be served. This became the basis for the angelic rebellion as the pride in their hearts was exposed, which God knew of beforehand.

Now think for a moment: if you had untold wealth and you were going to leave it as an inheritance, to whom would you leave it? Most of us would say to our spouse and children. However, if you do that, then you're only doing what anyone else would do. Therefore, if you're going to show your ability to love beyond measure, you have to love something that or someone who does not make sense in the natural order of family. This we call adoption.

When God informed the angels of His plan, Lucifer questioned His decision, saying that he was more like God than we were, reasoning that we are not qualified to be God's benefactors over His angels since they, not we, are more like Him. Therefore, the scriptures say that pride was found in him. Pride is simply thinking more of yourself than you really ought to. In his rebellion, Satan was able to convince one-third of the angels that God had made a mistake and that, in doing so, He was not God because it is impossible for God to be in error. Lucifer argued that they, the angels, should make him God instead so that they could become the beneficiaries of heaven. In doing so, they lost their place in heaven and were cast into outer darkness (which is the absence of the presence of God in the earthly realm of darkness). They are at war over this issue to this day.

It's interesting that if you study angels, you'll not see anywhere in scripture that angels have the ability to love or that they have the promise of being God's sons.[32] Therefore, let us examine some examples showing how God decides who will receive His promises. We'll start with Esau and Jacob. Esau was every father's dream son, and Jacob was a deceiver, but Esau made the same mistake Satan made: he did not value his position and subsequently lost his birthright because of his pride. Jacob was the younger, and even though he was not the heir, he obtained the inheritance because he fought for it, and God loved him for that. Consider next Ishmael and Isaac. Ishmael was the firstborn, but God chose Isaac over him.

When Israel needed a new judge, God called Gideon, who was the least of his family, the smallest family of the smallest clan of the smallest tribe.[33] Jacob, when he blessed his sons, crossed his hands and made Ephraim, Joseph's youngest son, the firstborn and the head of all the tribes[34] over his older brother Manasseh. David was the youngest of all his six other brothers. And look at Israel. Why did God choose them? The scriptures state that they were the least of all the nations. Have you ever heard of a nation of slaves besides Israel? How about the apostle Paul? He considered himself the least of all the believers because he persecuted the church. So, what's my point? You see that God always follows a divine protocol. He glorifies Himself when He redeems "the least of these" and demonstrates it in His ability to show extreme unmerited and unconditional love.

---

[32] Hebrews 1:4–5: "Being made so much better than the angels, as he hath by inheritance obtained a more excellent name than they. For to which of the angels said he at any time, thou art my Son, this day have I begotten thee? And again, I will be to him a Father, and he shall be to me a Son?"

[33] Judges 6:15: "And he said unto him, oh my Lord, wherewith shall I save Israel? behold, my family is poor in Manasseh, and I am the least in my father's house."

[34] Jeremiah 31:9: "They shall come with weeping, and with supplications will I lead them: I will cause them to walk by the rivers of waters in a straight way, wherein they shall not stumble: for I am a father to Israel, *and Ephraim is my firstborn*" (emphasis added).

But why is this important? Let's look at when God redeemed Israel and made them His people. In doing so, He disqualified the rest of us, because you're either a Jew or a Gentile; you're either the people of God or in the category of not being the people of God. He again shows His glory by making a way for the rest of us by grafting[35] us into the family. God chooses people not because they are deserving but rather because He loves unconditionally and is the great Redeemer (see John 3:16). Our part is to recognize and accept what He has done but then to produce a return on the investment He provided, for we must all stand before Him on day and give an account for our lives here in the earth.

Here is what we gain by understanding Ephesians 3:6: when the church learns to love the way God loves, even the fallen angels will know God's wisdom and will understand that He knew exactly what He was doing when He chose us over them. Until the church learns to do this, stops judging those on the outside, starts judging themselves, and loving those who are lost, they will never know the Jesus of scripture and the world will continue to hate Him because of our own poor behavior. If we are to be the bearers of the good news of the gospel, then we have to start behaving like the sons of our Father and not the Scribes and Pharisees of religion (which is one of the reasons the contemporary church model is powerless in terms of signs, wonders, and miracles). We are making the same mistake the Jews made. But while believers are looking for Christ to return, creation is waiting for us to become true sons (progenitors) of our Father.[36] Therefore, our goal as believers is to conform to the image of Jesus, the pattern Son, and represent God the way Jesus did. If the

---

[35] Ephesians 3:6: "That the Gentiles should be fellow heirs, and of the same body, and partakers of his promise in Christ by the gospel."

[36] Romans 8:19–21: "For the earnest expectation of the creature waiteth for the manifestation of the sons of God. For the creature was made subject to vanity, not willingly, but by reason of him who hath subjected the same in hope, Because the creature itself also shall be delivered from the bondage of corruption into the glorious liberty of the children of God."

world is waiting for this, then we need to stop judging them and start showing the love of God to the least of these, just like Jesus did.

Brother Tariq, even though it's been some time since I was there, I look forward to the day I will be with you again in Lahore. Hopefully we can continue the teachings to the benefit of those you minister to. Please send my regards to the pastors and your family as they were very kind to me while I was there. I found Pakistan to be an amazing place and the people there both extremely friendly and accommodating.

Blessings, Madson

The Human Condition—Driven by Our Adamic Nature

WHEN ADAM SINNED AND was disconnected from God, the scriptures say he knew he was naked. This came after he took and ate from the tree in the middle of the garden, the tree of the knowledge of good and evil. The knowledge of the tree of good and evil is not just the understanding of right and wrong; it is the knowledge of self-awareness. We were originally designed to be one with God. We were not designed to function apart from Him. You see, oneness with God is good, and to be separated from God is not the way we were designed to exist. Once we lost our symbiotic relationship, it caused a behavior modification that makes us operate in a way we were not designed for. You see, Adam, when he acquired this understanding, became aware that he had separated himself from the Lord through sin (sin is anything that separates you from God, not just the bad things you do), which is why the scripture says his eyes were opened and he knew he was naked. This awareness convinces us that because we are separated from God, we must now provide for ourselves that which was previously supplied by our inheritance as being part of His family. This was evident in that Adam tried to provide and protect himself—self-preservation. Neither of which he was successful at.

When God sought Adam in the garden, He asked him, "Who told you that you were naked?" In other words, the Lord wanted to know this: "Adam, who told you that you were less than what I created you to be?" This is the lie that we buy into. Our sense of self-preservation causes us to become self-reliant, and our sin nature then adopts Babylonian answers to solve our problems. Let me give you an example: When you were a child, your parents were your whole world. You had no concerns or worries in life because you trusted your parents for your every need. But when you became a teenager, you became aware of yourself apart from your parents. This is self-awareness. You understood you were your own person. Young people struggle through these years and often, like Adam, become rebellious. Hopefully in your later years you matured, and your perspective changed, and you then began to re-relate to your parents and restore the relationship.

This is why the scriptures declare that in Christ you have the right to become sons.[37] The whole goal of God is to restore us to our original fellowship with Him,[38] the same fellowship that we had with Him in the Garden of Eden, where the wealth of our Father was freely given to us. Isn't it interesting that Jesus overcame this issue of self-preservation in another garden, the garden of Gethsemane, before He was crucified and knew for the first time that He was without God's presence? Feeling abandoned in that garden, He said, Father, Father why hast thou forsaken me? And "If it be possible, let this cup pass from me: nevertheless, not as I will, but as thou wilt."[39]

---

[37] John 1:12: "But as many as received him, to them gave He power to become the sons of God" (KJV).

[38] John 17:9–11: "I pray for them: I pray not for the world, but for them which thou hast given me; for they are thine. And all mine are thine, and thine are mine; and I am glorified in them. And now I am no more in the world, but these are in the world, and I come to thee. Holy Father, keep through thine own name those whom thou hast given me, that they may be one, as we are."

[39] Luke 22:42: "Saying, Father, if thou be willing, remove this cup from me: nevertheless, not my will, but thine, be done."

The second example is this: When in our society we continue to separate ourselves from God, we suffer as a community and as a nation. Our effort to fix our society is an effort in self-preservation. As we try to repair our problems, the spirit of liberalism uses this to separate us from God, and our sense of self-preservation only causes us to increase our problems because the truth is that mankind needs to get back to God and reestablish a sense of biblical morality. God will then restore us as a people.[40] Because of this mind-set of self-preservation, many churches today have moved away from God's ordained governance of fivefold ministry (with the roles of apostle, prophet, evangelist, pastor, and teacher). This sense of self-preservation does not require the kind of faith that pleases God. And because we have the attitude that we must provide for ourselves, we've replaced fivefold ministry with business models and have conformed our churches to run like the systems of the world and not like the kingdom of our God. We've built pastoral pyramids to manage ever-changing and immature congregations with seeker-friendly church models that have no accountability but in turn offer us coffee and doughnuts and make us door greeters with vast programs to entertain our children but with little in the way of discipleship, which entails equipping and training believers for ministry. (the come as you are concept and remain as you are is contrary to transformational mandate to become Christ-like). These churches embrace ungodliness in order to stay relevant, and their only focus is easy evangelism. These church structures lack the strength of apostolic

> **Your destiny is determined by your participation. Your faith must have substance if you are to see the revelation of the kingdom at work on your behalf.**
> **Hebrews 11:1.**

---

[40] 2 Chronicles 7:14: "*If my people, which are called by my name, shall humble themselves, and pray, and seek my face, and turn from their wicked ways*; then will I hear from heaven, and will forgive their sin, and will heal their land" (emphasis added).

governance and prophetic sight that declares the kingdom of God to the principle spiritual strongholds that rules over our cities, states, and nations, so we attract crowds but experience little or no transformation. Many churches in the United States look more like community centers with their programs or even like country clubs with their activities, instead of looking like God's kingdom people who prevail against the gates (strongholds) of hell. Therefore, we operate in this basic tenet of fear, and we struggle to maintain our religious systems that God is constantly tearing down. If we want to see the power of God that transforms our cities, then we must replace our illegitimate and immature church structures and build His church His way. First Corinthians 12:27–28 clearly states that if you desire spiritual gifts, the strength to govern, help in ministry, miracles, and healings, then you must first have apostles, prophets, and teachers. Most of our churches have adopted pastoral and evangelistic models that do not have the foundation of apostolic governance or prophetic sight that is needed to properly establish a kingdom paradigm. Do not be like these churches. But develop your apostolic and prophetic grace with you focus on teaching and discipleship training.

God's answer to the problem is simple. Because of Adams sin, the curse we live under provides adversity in life we are to overcome. You see, it was not God's intention to punish Adam, but instead He cursed the ground and placed him under a standard of suffering in order to offset the self-reliance that Adam had acquired through the tree of the knowledge of good and evil. The suffering of the Christian is designed to make us once again dependent on God, who is faithful well beyond our own abilities, and build our confidence in Him. We can never hope to overcome an adversary who has distinct advantages over us unless we learn how to serve God unconditionally and not on our own strength. These truths ultimately gave Jesus the power to overcome as He was able to raise Himself from the impediment called death. When we, by our free will, overcome our sense of self-preservation, we will see our greatest miracles—and God's kingdom will advance in faith.

Understanding Monotheistic Religions

OF THE THREE MAJOR monotheistic religions, Judaism, Christianity and Islam—in other words, those religions that believe in the one God of Creation and whose adherents claim to be descendants of Abraham—the first, Judaism, believes in the God of Creation and believes that He is to be revered and worshipped, which Jewish people attempt to do by keeping the law. They too are waiting for the Messiah but have not accepted that He has already come. The second, Christianity, believes that Christians are not under the law but are under grace. Christians have accepted Jesus as the Christ the Messiah and through the church are the messengers of the good news of the gospel. Both the Jew and the Christian are after the spirit of Abel, but the Muslim is after the spirit of Cain. Muslims (believing that the third religion of Abraham being Islam) are a theonomous people in a heteronomous culture of works, whereas Christians and Jews are theonomous people under an autonomous culture and are shepherds. Therefore, the Christian and the Jew are in competition with the Muslim, and the Muslim's response is to kill his brother. Not only do Muslims desire death to people of other faiths who claim to serve God, but also, they desire the deaths of Muslims of other sects, as the Shi'a are in competition with the Sunnis to the point of violence. Muslims also believe they are the third and final expression of the people of God, believing that both the Jew and Christian have failed in their attempt to please God and that those who follow Islam are the rightful heirs of God, being that Ishmael was the firstborn of Abraham and that they are his descendants. References of both Jews and Christians are found in the Holy Bible, but Islam is only about sixteen hundred years old and is not found in biblical scripture except for a reference that Ishmael's descendants would become a great nation.[41] Therefore, Muslims have their own scriptures called the Koran. Many of its writings are contradictory to those found in the Holy Bible, all of which was written before Muhammad wrote the Koran. As revival continues to spread throughout the middle east, we welcome the millions of Muslims that are experiencing the freedom they're finding placing their faith in the Son of God, Jesus the Christ.

It's important to understand some basic tenets of each of these religions. It is not my intention to libel anyone but only to establish certain fundamental truths. The Christian's spiritual journey is to conform to the image of Jesus, the Son of God, and to undergo the spiritual birthing process that the apostle Paul referred to when discussing his spiritual upbringing as a Jew (which was considerable) as a time of security and spiritual growth, referring it as to a womb.[42] However, he came to understand that the revelation of Christ doesn't happen in your church. In other words, you need to leave the confines of your religious experience and go into the world, where the revelation of Christ in you might be fulfilled experientially.

Once I started down this path, I began to manifest the supernatural. In part, the church, being like a womb, is a place where God hides you from the enemy while you grow in grace. It is a place where you come under the governance of mentors and tutors whose goal is to

---

[41] Genesis 17:20: "And as for Ishmael, I have heard thee: Behold, I have blessed him, and will make him fruitful, and will multiply him exceedingly; twelve princes shall he beget, and I will make him a great nation."

[42] Galatians 1:15: "But when it pleased God, who separated me from my mother's womb, and called me by his grace, To reveal his Son in me, that I might preach him among the heathen; immediately I conferred not with flesh and blood."

release you into the inheritance that already belongs to you, but you have to qualify to receive your responsibility to manage it.[43] The church is not perfect, nor was it meant to be. It is a place to nurture the varying stages of your spiritual upbringing, designed to prepare you for the ministry God has destined you for. Therefore, everyone comes into Gods kingdom as a spiritual infant, who hopefully over time grows into a mature son or daughter. It is here you get equipped to represent your heavenly Father as a progenitor or extension of Him. And like Jesus, the pattern Son,[44] you have to learn how to do the works of your Father and, like Jesus, only do and say what you see and hear the Father doing and saying, all of which is accomplished through the indwelling of the Holy Spirit. The same Holy Spirit Jesus has, you have. Therefore, set your individual goal to grow and become Christ like in both the individual and the corporate sense as one who is an extension of God's will on the earth for the season in which you are here, and take on the purpose or destiny that He has for you outside the four walls of your church. The main hindrance is learning how to die to your Adamic nature.

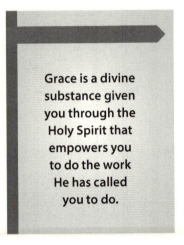

Grace is a divine substance given you through the Holy Spirit that empowers you to do the work He has called you to do.

---

[43] Galatians 4:1–7: "Now I say, That the heir, as long as he is a child, differeth nothing from a servant, though he be lord of all; But is under tutors and governors until the time appointed of the father. Even so we, when we were children, were in bondage under the elements of the world: But when the fulness of the time was come, God sent forth his Son, made of a woman, made under the law, To redeem them that were under the law, that we might receive the adoption of sons. And because ye are sons, God hath sent forth the Spirit of his Son into your hearts, crying, Abba, Father. Wherefore thou art no more a servant, but a son; and if a son, then a heir of God through Christ."

[44] 1 Timothy 1:16: "Howbeit for this cause I obtained mercy, that in me first Jesus Christ might show forth all longsuffering, for a pattern to them which should hereafter believe on him to life everlasting."

The self-preservation that guides you, is the same problem you have to overcome if you are to receive the promise, He has given you, which is why without faith it is impossible to please Him. Being yielded to the Holy Spirit and growing in grace[45] is key. God's grace comes to you in multiple expressions: salvation, prayer, Bible reading, participation, studying, mentoring (i.e., fathering), and performing acts of faith, to name a few.[46]

Now the pillars of Christianity are obedience, endurance, and faith. As you study the scriptures, you'll find there is a seldom talked about foundational covenant referenced by King David in 1 Chronicles 16:11–19:

> Seek the Lord and his strength, seek his face continually. Remember his marvelous works that he hath done, his wonders, and the judgments of his mouth; O ye seed of Israel his servant, ye children of Jacob, his chosen ones. He is the Lord our God; his judgments are in all the earth. Be ye mindful always of his covenant; the word which he commanded to a thousand generations; **Even of the covenant which he made with Abraham, and of his oath unto Isaac; And hath confirmed the same to Jacob for a law,** and to Israel for an everlasting covenant, Saying, Unto thee will I give the land of Canaan, the lot of your inheritance; When ye were but few, even a few, and strangers in it. 1 Chronicles 16:11-19 (KJV)

In order to understand the eternal covenant, we must study the lives of these three men (Abraham, Isaac, and Jacob) and their examples, which is the fabric of truth written in scripture. We, like them, must learn to carry the cross of Christ and in our walk

---

[45] Ephesians 3:18: "But grow in grace, and in the knowledge of our Lord and Savior Jesus Christ. To him be glory both now and forever. Amen."

[46] 1 Peter 4:10: "As every man hath received the gift, even so minister the same one to another, as good stewards of the manifold grace of God."

remembering the example of those who came before us. Abraham was obedient to the voice of God to the extent that he was willing to sacrifice his son. Isaac's covenant was built upon endurance as he was told to dwell in the land of Gerar (the place of contention). The people of the land declared that God was with him because he had endured unreasonable hardship while among the people of Gerar and had overcome. Jacob, having been a deceiver, became a man of faithfulness and eventually father to the twelve patriarchs, whom God used as a corporate example to teach us through their successes and failures. Through their story, we learn that we are held to account and that we have no excuses for how we conduct ourselves as we continue the journey in our own season.[47]

There has been a disproportionate emphasis on teaching faith within the church since the mid-1950s, and believers have struggled with acts of obedience and endurance as we have deviated from these foundational requirements. Many no longer understand how to carry their cross daily and have entered a period of easy believeism, at least here in the United States, where we see the "seeker friendly" church model that feeds, the consumer Christian mentality. The youth who have abandoned the faith of their forefathers no longer comprehend concepts like duty, consecration and holiness. Because the Pentecostal season had taught us how to be priestly, legalistic, and judgmental, when the charismatic season came and we began to understand the liberty of the believer, we lost our sense of holiness (each season has its strengths and weaknesses). Today the church must begin the process of relearning these virtues without the weaknesses of those seasons and inculcate a new expression of accuracy as the witnesses

---

[47] 1 Corinthians 10:1–6: "Moreover, brethren, I would not that ye should be ignorant, how that all our fathers were under the cloud, and all passed through the sea; And were all baptized to Moses in the cloud and in the sea; And did all eat the same spiritual meat; And did all drink the same spiritual drink: for they drank of that spiritual Rock that followed them: and that Rock was Christ. But with many of them God was not well pleased: for they were overthrown in the wilderness. Now these things were our examples, to the intent we should not lust after evil things, as they also lusted."

to the fullness of the expression of His love in all righteousness to a lost and dying world. Therefore, before we address the demonic hierarchy, let us examine our own inconsistencies whereby we may affect the appropriate change that will transform us into the people of God the way He designed us to be, in the image of His Son, who was sent as our example.

The Spiritual Dynamics of the Soul

FOR US TO UNDERSTAND what the redemption of our souls is all about its important that we understand the dynamics of our fallen state. We were created with a body, soul and a spirit. The body of flesh allows us to exist in a physical form and separates us from the spiritual realm. Our spirit is what animates our ability to function within our bodies, and our souls are the seat of our emotions. In our original design most theologians agree that our soul resides within our spirits which was connect to God and our spirit kept our emotions in check as our soul

> **The unlimited riches of heaven are reserved for those who are compliant to their calling, while the governments of men are based on taxing those, they claim to help**

was subjected to our spirits. In our fallen state our souls operate independent of our spirit. The reason once you are saved that you receive the Holy Spirit, is to create a path for you to reconnect with God all the while maintaining your free will. This is why it's important to study the scriptures and develop a prayer life with hopefully for most will also incorporate a prayer language (speaking in tongues, which is helpful but not mandatory) to assist you in developing a more intimate relationship with God. The reason so many in the world are emotional charged is that they allow their emotions to animate the flesh unchecked by their spirits because they know not God as either their father or the keeper of their souls. This also the reason most believers are conservative and the unredeemed look to government for their wellbeing because they are separated from God, who through Jesus Christ is the only path to finding true peace.

In this time of unrestricted social media access, information overload has driven civilization into emotional frenzy and given birth here in the US to groups like Antifa, Black Lives Matter, the rise of and resurgence of White Nationalism and Islam, all of which should be considered hate groups and have found their political expression within the Democratic party not only here in the United States but also abroad. This is also why reasonable thought and traditional values are cast aside because insecurity of the soul needs to be maintained at all cost at the expense of others. And why the church must demonstrate the love of God to this lost and dying generation, so that some will escape the wrath to come.

> 15 For that which I do I allow not: for what I would, that do I not; but what I hate, that do I. 16 If then I do that which I would not, I consent to the law that it is good. 17 Now then it is no more I that do it, but sin that dwelleth in me. 18 ***For I know that in me (that is, in my flesh,) dwelleth no good thing: for to will is present with me; but how to perform that which is good I find not. 19 For the good that I would I do not: but the evil which I would not, that I do. 20 Now if I do that I would not, it is no more I that do it, but sin that dwelleth in me. 21 I find then a law, that, when I would do good, evil is present with me. 22 For I delight in the law of God after the inward man: 23 But I see another law in my members, warring against***

the law of my mind, and bringing me into captivity to the law of sin which is in my members. 24 O wretched man that I am! who shall deliver me from the body of this death? 25 I thank God through Jesus Christ our Lord. So then with the mind I myself serve the law of God; but with the flesh the law of sin. Romans 7:15-25 (KJV)

And to esteem them very highly in love for their work's sake. And be at peace among yourselves. 14 Now we exhort you, brethren, warn them that are unruly, comfort the feebleminded, support the weak, be patient toward all men. 15 See that none render evil for evil to any man; but ever follow that which is good, both among yourselves, and to all men. 16 Rejoice evermore. 17 Pray without ceasing. 18 In every thing give thanks: for this is the will of God in Christ Jesus concerning you. 19 Quench not the Spirit. 20 Despise not prophesying's. 21 Prove all things; hold fast that which is good. 22 Abstain from all appearance of evil. 23 And the very God of peace sanctify you wholly; *and I pray God your whole spirit and soul and body be preserved blameless to the coming of our Lord Jesus Christ.* 24 Faithful is he that calleth you, who also will do it. 1st Thessalonians 5:13-24 (KJV)

Those Who Are Perishing

THERE ARE TWO TYPES of people on the earth, those who are being redeemed and those who have an unregenerate mind. And as I mentioned earlier, the latter is driven by our Adamic nature and the orphan mentality of self-preservation. Those who have not received in themselves the desire to reconnect with God will ultimately find themselves in rebellion against everything that is of God and what He has provided to establish His rule, order, and divine protocol concerning both the relationship aspects required to know Him and the kingdom dynamics that drive successful living. This sense of abandonment is what drives animosity toward the patriarchal system and promotes feminism, abortion, and rebellion against God divine protocol. Identity politics and the accompanying behavior is nothing more than what it's always been: people trying to find meaning in life. "Who am I? Why am I here? Is there a God? Does He care about me? Does He even know I exist?" We ask these questions because we were originally created as symbiotic beings. We were not created to function independently or apart from Him. Our sense of Fatherlessness and abandonment drives us to look for an alternative within the orphan mind-set we inherited from Adam that drives our need for identity. Some will find the truth of restored relationship through the redemptive power of the cross of Jesus Christ, by way of which we become part of the family of the children of God, thereby making us equals and heirs according to His promises.[48] This also gives us confidence by canceling out the orphan mentality we were born with. Others will turn to alternative religions, governmental oversight based on identity politics, gang membership, cause affiliation (environmentalism, etc.), group affiliation, homosexuality, drugs and alcohol, tattoos, piercings, and so forth, any means by which they may find group inclusion as a sense of identity. Again, this is all part of the Adversary's globalist goal of keeping us under his rule through collective control of government oversight through Socialist and ultimately Communist forms of government.

The national sense of modernism (which again is based on the societal embracing of Judeo-Christian values) has given way to postmodernism, which is the abandonment of these same values and a societal movement where everyone does what is right in their own eyes.[49] This primarily manifests in the political sphere as principalities and powers, and it works through political systems, influencing societal change toward the collective (socialist, communist, globalist) mind-set. Should this movement succeed and the whole of humanity embrace this paradigm, we will see the collapse of free societies, which will be followed by economic ruin across the globe. The demonic strategy is based on the destruction of the middle class whereby you have elitist party membership and a subservient class

---

[48] Galatians 3:26–29: "For ye are all the children of God by faith in Christ Jesus. For as many of you as have been baptized into Christ have put on Christ. There is neither Jew nor Greek, there is neither bond nor free, there is neither male nor female: for ye are all one in Christ Jesus. And if ye be Christ's, then are ye Abraham's seed, and heirs according to the promise."

[49] 2 Timothy 3:1–7: "This know also, that in the last days perilous times shall come. For men shall be lovers of their own selves, covetous, boasters, proud, blasphemers, disobedient to parents, unthankful, unholy, Without natural affection, trucebreakers, false accusers, incontinent, fierce, despisers of those that are good, Traitors, heady, high-minded, lovers of pleasures more than lovers of God; Having a form of godliness but denying the power thereof: from such turn away. For of this sort are they which creep into houses, and lead captive silly women laden with sins, led away with divers' lusts, Ever learning, and never able to come to the knowledge of the truth."

that fuels the prosperity of the elites but leaves the lower class in need and dependent on government programs which they themselves pay for through taxes. This is all fed by a covetous mentality as people surrender their freedoms for the fallacy that human governance can provide for them as a father provides for his family. Again, this is the orphan's thought process. The destruction of the middle class is necessary to eliminate any sense of hope or individual achievement that might challenge government rule.

After the Cold War with Russia, we saw a large part of the Russian population desirous to return to communism and the security it offered that they had become familiar with. The Russian people were willing to give up their newfound freedoms because they had become comfortable in a suppressive heteronomous culture where they had learned to survive but had little hope in the opportunities of a free people. They were much like the Israelites who longed for the provision they had while they were in Egypt[50] versus what awaited them in the unknown future as they tried to possess a land but were uncertain whether they would successfully come to own it. Consequently, a forty-year period of reformation through wilderness trials was necessary to cultivate a replacement theology of dependency on God instead of the servitude they'd given to the Egyptian pharaohs in order to achieve the objective of possessing the Promised Land, which included the death of the soldiers who were disobedient to the mandate in spite of the miracles they had just witnessed in having been recently delivered from Egypt.[51]

---

[50] Numbers 11:4–5, 20: "And the mixt multitude that was among them fell a lusting: and the children of Israel also wept again, and said, who shall give us flesh to eat? **We remember the fish, which we did eat in Egypt freely; the cucumbers, and the melons, and the leeks, and the onions, and the garlic**: ... But even a whole month, until it come out at your nostrils, and it be loathsome unto you: because that ye have despised the Lord which is among you, and have wept before him, saying, Why came we forth out of Egypt?"

[51] This the primary reason God does not operate solely dependently on the supernatural. The supernatural is still active, but historically it did not provide the motivation or confidence necessary to drive people forward. This is also

There are a few truths people need to understand about governments. First, governments have no money of their own; they collect taxes from their citizens or subjects. Second, governments are third-party payers. In other words, unlike us, they don't earn the money they spend. So, they often spend it wastefully. In every case when government competes with the private sector, the private sector outperforms because it operates as a free enterprise competition-driven system that we call capitalism. Capitalism is singularly the most productive system in human history that has advanced prosperity and relieved poverty on a global scale. The lie is that capitalism is based on greed, this could not be farther from the truth. The truth is that socialism, communism, and ultimately globalism is based on taking from those who have earned and giving it to those who have not (this is the definition of greed). Historically, capitalism is a superior system. So why is there such unrest among our youth and a rejection of established truth within the millennial culture? Frankly it's because our adversary has undermined our culture over time and used governmental control, and social engineering to propagate the lie that the freedoms we have, haven't provided for their future (i.e., that we didn't build it ourselves) and the belief that the millennials' parents had in marriage, family, and faith never delivered on the promises they were told as children. It's an understakable conclusion based on the government's deflection of responsibility away from a nationalist mandate of the sovereignty of a country toward a globalist agenda of elitist control. Blaming others for economic and social upheaval while our leaders intentionally continue to dissolve the culture that built the prosperity, we enjoy here in the United States, it is the spirit of covetousness. This is why the leftist, liberal Paradigm promotes the reversal of Western culture, because a theonomous culture in an autonomous society empowers individualism and the entrepreneurial paradigm that fuels economic growth and challenges governmental rule.

---

why we must emphasize relationship and discipleship in this season if we are to operate successfully as progenitors or sons and daughters of God.

I live in a strong economic community, and one thing I see is that when people have a decent income, their victimization mentality is minimal. In other words, racism, sexism, victimhood, and marginalization is almost nonexistent when people prosper. If there was ever a privileged class of people, it would not be the white people of the United States but would be American privilege, for all Americans (of all races). No other country provides you with as much opportunity to succeed or fail than the United States, regardless of your ethnicity, color, or gender. Therefore, we see principalities working through liberal government to drive debt up and increase government dependency, which gives the elites more control, while driving down the quality of life and ultimately leading us away from the kingdom principles that drive successful living and the universal principles built into creation, like the law of the harvest[52] or what is commonly referred to as the law of attraction. Know this: whenever you align yourself with biblical truth and its benefits, you'll prosper when you keep to those truths, and conversely when you're out of alignment, you struggle. It's all about compliancy. Therefore, guard your hearts as you minister, stay focused on God's truths, and don't conform to the image of the world, because it will feed your Adamic tendencies and you'll find yourself questioning God and His principles. I'll write to you on the authenticity of what it means to be a believer soon, which is a conversation for another time.

> Whenever you align yourself with biblical truth and its benefits, you'll prosper when you keep to those truths, and conversely when you're out of alignment, you struggle. It's all about compliancy

---

[52] Mark 4:24: "And he said to them, Take heed what ye hear: with what measure ye mete, it shall be measured to you: and to you that hear shall more be given" (KJV).

Currently my main emphasis is on the condition of church and its advancement against the gates of hell. The church does not seem to have a global voice it should be using to herald the advancement of Gods kingdom and demonstrate its prophetic authority to speak on behalf of God as it was designed to do. The church in the previous seasons of Protestant, Pentecostalism and the Charismatic has fallen into the same state as Joshua, not knowing how to finish its assignment. Therefore, the current voice of the church will soon make a noticeable shift in its expression as new leadership from an apostolic paradigm emerges, replacing the evangelical sound that has mostly focused on the salvation aspects of the gospel message and God's heart for the lost, but not on discipleship or equipping the saints as the voice of the coming kingdom of God. Jesus faced the same dilemma in His day, which you can read about in Matthew 10 and 11. But the signs of this season will be relationships, restoration of teaching and discipleship through spiritual fathering and ministry alliances over networking.

Preaching the Wrong Message

The ministry of John the Baptist and his salvation message gave way to the kingdom message of Jesus, which came in power.[53] For with each new season, the previous one must decrease. This current shift will be hallmarked by the revelation of a mature church able to do all things as it finds a new sense of unity and purpose and begins an outward expression in the similitude of Jesus as sons (progenitors) of our heavenly Father.[54] As God moves us through seasons from

---

[53] Romans 8:18–19: "For I reckon that the sufferings of this present time are not worthy to be compared with the glory which shall be revealed in us. For the earnest expectation of the creature waiteth for the manifestation of the sons of God."

[54] Ephesians 4:11–16: "And he gave some, apostles; and some, prophets; and some, evangelists; and some, pastors and teachers; For the perfecting of the saints, for the work of the ministry, for the edifying of the body of Christ: *Till we all come in the unity of the faith, and of the knowledge of the Son of God, to a*

glory to glory, the problem is that if we do not advance to the new thing God is revealing, we'll find ourselves opposed to the will of God and the next expression He's adding to the church—much like the Ephraimites did to the tribe of Judah when they lost their firstborn privilege after the mandate was taken from them and given to the tribe of Judah[55] under Caleb. Much of the book of Hosea is a written reproach against Ephraim and how they treated Judah when they received the mandate to lead and complete the assignment that Joshua had been given. We must always remember that the Lord knows the times and season of His doings,[56] and we do not. If we fail to do our part, then we run the risk of becoming like John the Baptist, judging the wrong person, being imprisoned, having our ministry shut down, and eventually losing our life, all because we didn't walk in obedience and decrease so that the new season with its additional benefits could manifest unhindered by the old. As the church of God, we must be careful not to judge new moves and seasons against those times when we memorialized what He did in past seasons as an end-all simply because we experienced something new. There is always a past season, a current season, and those seasons that are yet to come. (My position is that we are in the last season, which is the gathering of the divided church in waves as we come to the unity of the faith.) It is for all of us to walk humbly in

---

perfect man, to the measure of the stature of the fulness of Christ: That we henceforth be no more children, tossed to and fro, and carried about with every wind of doctrine, by the sleight of men, and cunning craftiness, whereby they lie in wait to deceive; But speaking the truth in love, may grow up into him in all things, which is the head, even Christ: From whom the whole body fitly joined together and compacted by that which every joint supplieth, according to the effectual working in the measure of every part, maketh increase of the body to the edifying of itself in love" (emphasis added).

[55] Judges 1:1–2: "Now after the death of Joshua it came to pass, that the children of Israel asked the Lord, saying, Who shall go up for us against the Canaanites first, to fight against them? And the Lord said, Judah shall go up: behold, I have delivered the land into his hand."

[56] Acts 1:7: "And he said to them, It is not for you to know the times or the seasons, which the Father hath put in his own power."

our season and be responsible for our generation's learning from the previous season, all the while looking forward to the next level of glory that will come and the ability to transform into the fullness of it. Therefore, be patient with the leaders in your territory. Let them see your humility, purity, and love in doing good works and the wisdom that is coming toward you as God establishes you there in Pakistan as a gateway church that is ushering in the things of the new season, always encouraging them in kingdom's dynamics with demonstrations of power and authority and with boldness, yet in love.

I will write to you again soon. May the Lord keep you and prosper you in every way.

Blessings. Madson

The Time of the Removal of Restraint

Now we request you, brethren, with regard to the coming of our Lord Jesus Christ and our gathering together to Him, that you not be quickly shaken from your composure or be disturbed either by a spirit or a message or a letter as if from us, to the effect that the day of the Lord has come. Let no one in any way deceive you, for it will not come unless the apostasy comes first, and the man of lawlessness is revealed, the son of destruction, who opposes and exalts himself above every so-called god or object of worship, so that he takes his seat in the temple of God, displaying himself as being God. Do you not remember that while I was still with you, I was telling you these things? And you know what restrains him now, so that in his time he will be revealed. For the mystery of lawlessness is already at work; <u>only he who now restrains will do so until he is taken out of the way.</u> Then that lawless one will be revealed whom the Lord will slay with the breath of His mouth and bring to an end by the appearance of His coming; that is, the one whose coming is in accord with the activity of Satan, with all power and signs and false wonders, and with all the deception of wickedness for those who perish, because they did not receive the love of the truth so as to be saved. For this reason, God will send upon them a deluding influence so that they will believe what is false, in order that they all may be judged who did not believe the truth but took pleasure in wickedness. (2 Thessalonians 2:1–12 NASB)

WE HAVE IN RECENT times seen a propagation of the removal of restraint manifest as principalities realign themselves against the advancement of God's kingdom of righteousness. The alignment of the global socialist movement has been interrupted as God has intervened in the affairs of mankind in what the scriptures call "the time of the removal of the one who restrains." In this time, the conviction of the Holy Spirit has been diminished from the landscape of human thought, leaving only the condemnation of the adversary speaking to the Adamic nature of the souls of mankind. This is the great delusion of the last days when human beings will be left unto themselves and the error of their ways as the impact of the removal of biblical morality engulfs the nations. As the nations are being measured, the church will be the refuge that the sanity of mankind will seek out. Civilization is at a crossroads where God has allowed us to deal with issues that He had previously contained through a sense of prevailing morality that had held influence over mankind within cultural norms through established governments

> The removal of the one who provided restraint came, with the introduction of smartphone technology, which ushered in access to instant global communication and information. This technology is the equivalent of the, Tower of Babel.

but that have recently been abandoned as the spirit of lawlessness has infiltrated societies since the early 1990s, of which we are now seeing the effects. We see the rise of black money from small businesses in the form of street money, along with income from other nontaxed business models like illegal immigration, sex trafficking, and illegal drugs. This has created a global financial crisis as governments must deal with diminishing tax revenues in order to maintain viable systems of infrastructure, which is causing dangerous shifts in established laws as the removal of restraint spreads. We see places in the United States like California implement Democratic progressive socialist systems as the adversary restructures his Babylonian program, which will eventually take us into a communist globalist system, of which the socialist paradigm shift is just the first step. This shift, if left unchecked, will plunge the world into unmanageable poverty, leaving a caste system with a lower class and elitist rule. Our best current example of this is China, where millions are displaced, put in internment camps, and even murdered because freedom-seeking people within are finding faith the Son of God, making the church a threat to the subjugation of government rule. In spite of this Christianity's growth in China is out pacing all other nations and is poised to be have the largest Christian population of any nation over the next ten to fifteen years. This will be a problem for the Communist Government as God kingdom advances to become the preeminent religion in China and begins to challenge the ruling principalities there.

As I mentioned earlier, South America's failing socialist economies are all now hanging in the balance, either they reembrace the autonomous capitalist paradigm by which they once prospered or, like Cuba, turning to communism as a method to maintain control. The recent acceptance of the Cuban government by the United States' previous administration was an attempt to normalize this type of culture in the minds of Americans. I watched this in South Africa as the heteronomous system of the government of apartheid—white rule—was dismantled by the emerging leadership of Nelson Mandela and his contemporaries as they struggled for assistance and almost turned toward communism. Had the United States not reversed its position and embraced them as an emerging democracy, South Africa would have most certainly had a civil war. But still, even today, the corruption of the South African government has opened the possibility of an emerging communist government, which is why Christians must remain vigilant there. If it were not for the apostolic voice of the church there, I would have no hope for the redemption of South Africa as a nation.

Ultimately mankind must decide whom they will serve. Will they submit to the righteous rule of God through His Christ, Jesus, the only righteous King, or will they choose a Babylonian alternative? Each generation must also decide whom they will serve in their season, knowing full well their choice will affect their sons and daughters in the next generation. For these things are introduced over long periods of time so that people are more easily deceived as the consequences of their choices are minimized through the subtle introduction of these systems. However, concerning this time of the removal of the one who restrains, it is a place marker in time, and the Lord is intervening in the affairs of men because mankind in and of themselves do not have the capacity to rule righteously over themselves. Therefore, we can never achieve God's desire for us without Him, and without Him all governments of mankind will fail until Jesus establishes His kingdom here on earth. The removal of restraint marks a season on God's timeline when mankind will come to an end of itself in regard to whom it will submit to.

I believe the new progressive leftist agenda, which clearly stands against the rule of God in favor of the elitist rule of man,[57] has made subtle gains over the last few decades but is now being dismantled. As recently as 2016 we've seen a new administration rise in the United States that has stood against the globalist movement. Along with the United Kingdom's exit from the European Union, Brexit, the European globalist union is being dismantled, a major shift as North Korea is coming into the community of free nations. Iran will

---

[57] That is, a heteronomous government.

follow suit as the people there are making sacrifices for autonomous change. In France the environmental climate change agenda (which is the spirit of Ashtoreth, a power, i.e., *exousia*) is being rejected as has been happening in the United States. The failing socialism of South America has driven a migration to the United States that is unprecedented as people are desperately seeking survival from those oppressive systems of government. Ultimately the United States will build a barrier wall to deal with the illegal immigration problem, allowing more people to assimilate into the country legally. Even in Pakistan your new prime minister is a nationalist progressive leader in the vein of the global reformation that is returning the country to a modernist culture. These are all signs of God's intervention and the fulfillment of Isaiah 2,[58] along with the fulfillment of scripture in that the meek are inheriting the earth. During this time, as the world is now in unhindered rebellion against the kingdom of God, the power of the adversary, who has worked within the boundaries of established governmental authority, has been derailed by the breakdown of these systems, governments that at one time, even though they are not religious organizations, followed biblical principles as a guideline to manage cultural morality. Our adversary uses established measurable systems to promote his agenda and control mankind while attempting to postpone God's established rule over the coming kingdom of righteousness.[59]

---

[58] Isaiah 2:2–5: "And it shall come to pass in the last days, that the mountain of the Lord's house shall be established in the top of the mountains, and shall be exalted above the hills; and all nations shall flow unto it. And many people shall go and say, Come ye, and let us go up to the mountain of the Lord, to the house of the God of Jacob; and he will teach us f his ways, and we will walk in his paths: for out of Zion shall go forth the law, and the word of the Lord from Jerusalem. And he shall judge among the nations and shall rebuke many people: and they shall beat their swords into plowshares, and their spears into pruninghooks: nation shall not lift up sword against nation, neither shall they learn war any more. O house of Jacob, come ye, and let us walk in the light of the Lord."

[59] Hebrews 1:8: "But to the Son he saith, Thy throne, O God, is for ever and ever: a sceptre of righteousness is the sceptre of thy kingdom."

The first principle you must understand is the corporeal principle, in which celestial beings must have human participation in order to translate their will and manifest their desires on the earth. Through your consciousness, the Holy Spirit communicates to your spirit the things concerning God's will for you so that you may carry out His will on the earth. Summarily, our adversary is doing the same by attempting to control mankind through access to the soul. These efforts to manipulate us are both individually subtle and built into the fabric of societal control. Remember—I first spoke of principalities (*arche*) working through the three cultural paradigms, explaining how powers (*exousia*) work through government systems. The third-level rulers of darkness (*kosmokrator-skotos*) are subsystems that include entertainment, sports, education, and media control. These are some of the systems our adversary uses to manipulate our social consciousness. God in His wisdom has today, much like He did in Moses's day, allowed the people in the land of Canaan to establish an infrastructure so that He could give the land to His people as an inheritance. They subdued an inferior system and reaped the benefits of it, ultimately conforming it to God's kingdom design. This process took over four hundred years to accomplish, culminating in the conquering of the land by King David.[60] This was necessary to overcome the systems of the world before God's kingdom could be established in its fullness (God is not interested in cohabitation with the kingdom of darkness). The scriptures declare that the kingdoms of the earth must become the kingdom of our God.[61]

---

[60] 1 Chronicles 22:17–19: "David also commanded all the princes of Israel to help Solomon his son, saying, *Is not the* Lord *your God with you? and hath he not given you rest on every side? for he hath given the inhabitants of the land into mine hand; and the land is subdued before the* Lord, *and before his people. Now set your heart and your soul to seek the* Lord *your God; arise therefore, and build ye the sanctuary of the* Lord God, *to bring the ark of the covenant of the* Lord, *and the holy vessels of God, into the house that is to be built to the name of the* Lord" (emphasis added).

[61] Revelation 11:15: "And the seventh angel sounded; and there were great voices in heaven, saying, The kingdoms of this world are become the kingdoms of our Lord, and of his Christ; and he shall reign for ever and ever."

During this season of the removal of restraint, we're seeing the first of these systems crumble, namely, what has been called fake media. Public trust in both national and local news outlets has been replaced by trust in the internet and social media as the daily display of information propagated by mainstream media is being discredited and the public is starting to understand the depths of the deception that has been propagated by a global assault on God's truth by an elitist element within governments to manipulate and control the will of the people, the depths of which have not been revealed until now. None of this was possible until the advent of smartphone technology. These entrenched systems will continue to be uncovered as God moves ahead of us to destroy the works of our adversary, much like He destroyed the city of Jericho, tearing down the walls so that His people could take the city. In conjunction with this, we're seeing the dismantling of the Roman circus[62] since the gateway to our soul is our Adamic nature, a nature of self-preservation where protection and provision is our operating system and the lust of the eyes, the lust of the flesh, the pride of life, and the spirit of covetousness fuel our every desire.

The Roman circus represents the distraction of the people from the things of God through the pride of life and through the lens of entertainment. The removal of the distraction of professional sports is another earmark of this season. We're watching the fabric of society being permanently altered as entrenched systems of control are being systematically diminished during this time. As God is redeeming the time for His purposes, He continues to intervene in the affairs of mankind for our good. The issue of professional

---

[62] The Roman circus is a reference to the Roman government's use of the sports arena to distract the people from the politics of the day. Our current form of government in the form of a democratic republic borrows much of its structure from this example. While we have a constitutional republic, the Roman government was based on the will of the emperors and eventually became tyrannical in its operation. The deception of public awareness eventually caused the deterioration of the republic, which led to its downfall as the republic gave way to empirical rule.

sports is not that God cares about you watching or playing football, soccer, golf, cricket, etc., but that these things steal your time and take time away from your pursuit of Him. This is the modern-day version of idolatry, and it's one of the Ten Commandments[63] not to put anything before God. Hopefully people will redirect their time into having a day devoted to the worship of God, family, and rest.

Among the more measurable shifts we can currently see is what's happening in our political system, demonstrated by celestial warfare over the souls of mankind for the future of not only the United States but also the entire world. Will we submit to the principality of the socialist agenda of control where government dictates our moral prerogatives and the globalist agenda, forfeiting the freedoms we have for the false hope of man-made government security, or will we reembrace the moral fiber of scripture, willfully recognizing the sovereignty of God, which calls us to be His progenitors and become more like a Jesus, the pattern Son,[64] willing extensions of Him, knowing that our privilege of free will and choice comes with consequences that we have little to no control over as we reap what we sow in this life? Because of this, we should be sober-minded, redeeming the time to the best of our ability. Unfortunately, what we've done is to have followed the example of ancient Israel in that we have chosen to reject the rule of God through His prophets and have chosen earthly kings like Saul to rule over us. These leaders are charismatically appealing but operate from the Adamic nature. In the previous US election, we voted for a man who appeared to have the attributes that would redefine and improve us as a people. Instead he declared that we we're not a Christian nation but that we should embrace a globalist paradigm and surrender our rights to a greater purpose. He was a man of insecurity, having grown up

---

[63] Exodus 20:1–3: "And God spake all these words, saying, I am the Lord thy God, which have brought thee out of the land of Egypt, out of the house of bondage. Thou shalt have no other gods before me."

[64] 1 Timothy 1:16: "Howbeit for this cause I obtained mercy, that in me first Jesus Christ might show forth all longsuffering, for a pattern to them which should hereafter believe on him to life everlasting."

fatherless, raised by his grandparents after his mother's death. He identified with an African culture that has also struggled to find purpose because they choose to identify with their ancestral past, not embracing the opportunity of our autonomous US culture, but rather embracing a victim paradigm, which is the spirit of covetousness. I find it interesting that of all the various ancestral people groups that make up the United States, African Americans, in their desire for identity, struggle to embrace the fact that they are no more African than anyone else whose ancestors came here from other cultures to embrace an identity that they could not have had where they came from. My ancestors were mainly from Europe, and while I'm an American, I identify as a son of the kingdom of God living in the United States (a Christian theonomous person in an autonomous culture).

The liberal agenda in the form of the Democratic Party is losing power now that the black community is realizing they have been victims of the party they thought would recognize and empower them. Instead it has used them to further an agenda that takes away the freedom of those who embrace it in exchange for the promise of a false security. Now that the liberal, progressive Democrats are victimizing the Hispanic community, Mexican Americans are adopting the African American victim role in the political arena. This too will ultimately fail as most Hispanics are Catholic and have fled the socialist governments of their South American countries. I find it interesting that my Hispanic friends who are in the United States legally are extremely conservative and to some extent far more righteous in their lifestyle than most American Christians and the people of other ethnicities in our communities. But those who are trying to come here illegally are, in their desperation, willingly accepting the consequences of their actions in being loyal to the Democratic Party in exchange for the promise of a freedom they can never have under that system. Because no matter how hard they try, man-made government will never have the answers that the world needs. These things are only found in Jesus Christ and His kingdom, which is literally the only example of what scripture calls a city on a hill and a light in the darkness. Therefore, our loyalties are to be to the lifestyle of the kingdom of righteousness and its biblical mandates, which supersede those of the place where we reside.[65]

Our previous president here in the United States failed to identify with God's kingdom but embraced the fatherless mentality of the orphan and sought to change the culture where the government takes responsibility for each citizen's well-being. This is the plan of our adversary, to keep us dependent on worldly man-made systems of control so that the kingdoms of this earth do not become the kingdom of our God. Therefore, we've elected charismatic, narcissistic leaders because they appear to be confident in themselves in their outward appearance. This is the deception; they identify not with God but, because of their insecurities, identify with a replacement figure in the form of government as the caretaker of their souls. The unregenerate mind does not comprehend the things that identify with faith in God or the principles of the kingdom because these are contrary to the desires of the flesh, in which such a mind has placed its hope. Therefore, in the material world, the Adamic nature's impulse to provide for and protect oneself prevails, and the identity of faith is ridiculed. This is also a sign of what happens when people who do seemingly good things but think they able to stand before God, all the while denying the One who is able to save them, which is evident in their works, disguised by their words. These are those people who need other human beings to see their works and validate them in this life. However, when they are judged, it will become apparent that they never knew Jesus or the power of the resurrection as children of God. Instead, they had a never-ending desire for validation that was never quenched, so they awarded themselves accolades and constantly endeavored to be recognized for the good that they did,

---

[65] Romans 2:13–15: "For not the hearers of the law are just before God, but the doers of the law shall be justified. For when the Gentiles, which have not the law, *do by nature the things contained in the law, these, having not the law, are a law to themselves*: Which show the work of the law written in their hearts, their conscience also bearing witness, and their thoughts the mean while accusing or else excusing one another" (emphasis added).

never understanding that dying to self and humility are the marks of a true disciple. Therefore, they embrace sin as a path to position, not understanding that Jesus suffered and died not to validate our sin but to deliver us from sin—something government cannot offer, because the orphan's need is what fuels dependence on the governments of mankind and empowers the government as a father figure.

> Beware of false prophets, who come to you in sheep's clothing, but inwardly they are ravening wolves. Ye shall know them by their fruits: Do men gather grapes from thorns, or figs from thistles? Even so every good tree bringeth forth good fruit; but a corrupt tree bringeth forth evil fruit. A good tree cannot bring forth evil fruit, neither can a corrupt tree bring forth good fruit. Every tree that bringeth not forth good fruit is hewn down and cast into the fire. Wherefore by their fruits ye shall know them, Not everyone that saith to me, Lord, Lord, shall enter into the kingdom of heaven; but he that doeth the will of my Father who is in heaven. Many will say to me in that day, Lord, Lord, have we not prophesied in thy name? and in thy name have cast out demons? and in thy name done many wonderful works? And then will I profess to them, I never knew you: depart from me, ye that work iniquity. (Matthew 7:15–23 KJV)

We are at the point where God must intervene in order to bring about the fruition[66] of His plan; otherwise, the whole world will be

---

[66] 2 Thessalonians 2:7–10: "For the mystery of iniquity doth already work: only he who now letteth will let, until he be taken out of the way. And then shall that Wicked be revealed, whom the Lord shall consume with the spirit of his mouth, and shall destroy with the brightness of his coming: Even him, whose coming is after the working of Satan with all power and signs and lying wonders, And with all deceivableness of unrighteousness in them that perish; because they received not the love of the truth, that they might be saved."

subjected to the globalist agenda to dominate mankind and suppress the work of the church. It is the goal of principalities and powers to eliminate the church where it can, and where it can't to put it under state control. This is evident in the communist paradigm that the prince of this world, through the state-run government, uses to control God's people, to the extent that it becomes of no effect and the path toward the restoration of mankind into correct fellowship with our heavenly Father becomes significantly hindered. We could if we so chose, move into a period of global darkness before we experience a spiritual renaissance. My personal belief is that the timeline is such that this will not be the case, that a counter shift against humanity's rule is clearly taking place, even though it's being under acknowledged. And the church is silent about it because God is moving sovereignly at this time as He intervenes in the affairs of mankind.

When Israel rejected Samuel as God's chosen representative for Saul, who looked as if he could take on the role of king, they were both warned as to what would happen to them as a people. Saul refused to go to Gilgal and be taught how to rule as a spokesperson for God until he found himself facing defeat by the Philistines[67]

---

[67] 1 Samuel 10:8–9, 12–15: "And thou shalt go down before me to Gilgal; and, behold, I will come down unto thee, to offer burnt offerings, and to sacrifice sacrifices of peace offerings: seven days shalt thou tarry, till I come to thee, and shew thee what thou shalt do. And ye have this day rejected your God, who himself saved you out of all your adversities and your tribulations; and ye have said unto him, Nay, but set a king over us. Now therefore present yourselves before the Lord by your tribes, and by your thousands. ... And when ye saw that Nahash the king of the children of Ammon came against you, ye said unto me, Nay; *but a king shall reign over us: when the* Lord *your God was your king.* Now therefore behold the king whom ye have chosen, and whom ye have desired! and, behold, the Lord hath set a king over you. If ye will fear the Lord, and serve him, and obey his voice, and not rebel against the commandment of the Lord, then shall both ye and also the king that reigneth over you continue following the Lord your God: But if ye will not obey the voice of the Lord, but rebel against the commandment of the Lord, then shall the hand of the Lord be against you, as it was against your fathers" (emphasis added).

two years later, but by then it was too late. (Thamo Naidoo's book on Gilgal is a must-read for everyone called to minister as each of us must learn how to function in our assignments if we are to maximize or efforts in ministry.) Saul violated divine protocol in the initial stages of his calling, and because of this he ruled from a place of insecurity for the next fifteen years, ultimately becoming the example for David of how not to rule. David, while he had been anointed king, was given a season to learn from Saul's mistakes. This, along with Samuel's instructions, helped groom him so that at the proper time he could fulfill God's will to possess the land. This also demonstrates both God's sovereignty and mankind's free will as God, who originally gave mankind rule over the earth to possess it, allowed the voices of the people to determine their own destiny even though it wasn't His will for them.[68] Therefore, understand that everything men chose by their free-will isn't necessarily God's will.

In ancient days God established kings, but in our culture, we elect representatives. It is a great responsibility and privilege in those countries where we have these republican and democratic principles given to us. It is also a great disappointment that in countries like the United States, where Christians dominate the population, they have chosen not to take responsibility for their city, state, and federal governments and have voted in godless leaders, having bought into the lie that we should separate ourselves from government when it's clear that Christians could own this country for God, if we would only participate and not abdicate our role in possessing the land for God. Again, Christians have been deceived by these celestial lies. The American church has been bought out by way of the 501(c)(3) designation, and we are forced to keep politics out of our pulpits for the promise of financial gain. I look forward to the day when we shake that bondage and can start preaching righteousness in spite of the cultural influences that hinder God's purposes. Tariq, we will

---

[68] 1 Samuel 8:7: "And the Lord said unto Samuel, Hearken unto the voice of the people in all that they say unto thee: for they have not rejected thee, but they have rejected me, that I should not reign over them."

continue to see a plumb line in this season as nations are measured in the sight of mankind and the removal of restraint continues to expose the works of the adversary. In the future you will see continuing global pushback against nationalism as the meek rise up against the elites of this world to reclaim their right to control their own destiny. It is one of God's universal principles built into Creation that drives all mankind toward His eternal desire to have heirs through whom He can reveal His majesty to those who desire to willingly worship Him in spirit and in truth (His truth).

There are various expressions of the removal of restraint that I have not gone into in great detail, but in a broader sense I have tried to lay some foundations by which we as Christians can come into a commonality of purpose in our understanding of the times we live in and of the responsibilities that face us as the grace of God has narrowed in this time. This season is about a plumb line being established on the earth, and people must choose whom they will serve, the gods of this world, which lead to destruction, or the God who created this world and reaches out with His love to all those who freely accept His gift of redemption. At this time, God in His wisdom has removed the boundaries that have made His grace toward men freely accessible in that a generation has risen up that has rejected His kindness, mercy, and love.[69] We as believers are now called to be more active participants for the Lord in requiring a just recompense for the suffering and death of His Son on our behalf. The evangelical paradigm of the easy believeism of the seeker-friendly church is

---

[69] John 3:16–21: "For God so loved the world, that he gave his only begotten Son, that whoever believeth in him should not perish, but have everlasting life. For God sent not his Son into the world to condemn the world; but that the world through him might be saved. He that believeth on him is not condemned: but he that believeth not is condemned already, because he hath not believed in the name of the only begotten Son of God. And this is the condemnation, that light is come into the world, and men loved darkness rather than light, because their deeds were evil. *For everyone that doeth evil hateth the light, neither cometh to the light, lest his deeds should be reproved. But he that doeth truth cometh to the light, that his deeds may be made manifest, that they are wrought in God*" (emphasis added).

not sufficient to maintain or advance the kingdom in its fullness; therefore, change is required. Whether we agree with this concept or not, there is a new line in the sand by which we must hold ourselves accountable for the work of God in this generation. The question is simple: what will you allow God to do in your life today that is an honest expression of the price that was paid for your salvation?[70]

Tariq my friend. I will write again as time allows. Greet everyone for me and pray that I may come to you in the near future.

Blessings. Madson

---

[70] 1 Corinthians 6:18–20: "What? know ye not that your body is the temple of the Holy Spirit which is in you, which ye have of God, What? know ye not that your body is the temple of the Holy Spirit which is in you, which ye have of God, and ye are not your own? *For ye are bought with a price: therefore, glorify God in your body, and in your spirit, which are God's*" (emphasis added).

Principalities and Powers

THE DEMONIC HIERARCHY IS made up of principalities, powers, rulers of darkness, and spiritual wickedness in high places, each of which serve a distinctive role in the kingdom of darkness. Some of the most notable characteristics of principalities is that they appeal to the orphan mind-set because they mirror the same position and are therefore relatable. Jupiter, Zeus and Thor, among others, are offspring of their deceased fathers, Saturn, Cronus and Odin, respectively. All of them rule from a heavenly position, and as defenders of mankind, they position themselves as replacement father figures that appeal to the desire in mankind for protection and provision, which is inherent in our Adamic nature. The distraction is that their fathers are gone, and they have replaced them, and therefore God, whom we know as our heavenly Father, is not attainable, so we must choose from among these false gods to fulfill our needs. Jesus does not offer Himself as a substitute for God but rather reveals Himself as our brother and in doing so shows us the way back to a relationship with our Father, our Creator, as a pattern Son. Neither does He rule over us from a heavenly position but rules within our hearts when we accept Him as our Redeemer and willfully submit to the rules of the kingdom as we seek that standard first to meet our needs.[71]

---

[71] Matthew 6:32–33: "(For after all these things do the Gentiles seek) for your heavenly Father knoweth that ye have need of all these things. **But seek ye**

As I mentioned, I will not go into all of the false gods at this time, but I would like to mention a few because they are so prevalent in the world, and many are deceived into following them. I am mainly concerned with how many Christians have willfully accepted these spirits into their lives, thereby fulfilling the scripture that if it were possible, even the elect would be deceived. In the near future we will see how these strongholds have influenced our government leaders as the Lord is going to expose them for the world to see.

Baal (a principality/*arche*) is a god that is half bull and half man. For the purpose of this chapter, I'll refer to Baal as the "spirit of the age," which is about self and humanism whereby mankind creates God in its own image, which distorts the glory that was mankind's, made in the image of God. In the Old Testament, the Israelites were warned by God to abstain from the worship of Baal, the god of this world, who through child sacrifice offered prosperity for good harvests, gold, brass, good weather, etc. He was also known in other cultures as Jupiter, Zeus, Gaia, Beelzebub, Mazda, and Amon of Egypt, to name a few of the more commonly known heathen gods. The Israelites were continually warned not to engage in the types of worship that included sex with relatives or children, sex with one's neighbor's spouse, child sacrifice, abortion and bestiality, which the scriptures call an abomination. The scriptures also say these things represent a state of confusion (i.e., mental illness), which, it is safe to say, is inclusive of all these unnatural behaviors.

> And the Lord spake unto Moses, saying, speak unto the children of Israel, and say unto them, I am the Lord your God. After the doings of the land of Egypt, wherein ye dwelt, shall ye not do: and after the doings of the land of Canaan, whither I bring you, shall ye not do: neither shall ye walk in their ordinances. Ye shall do my judgments, and keep mine ordinances,

---

first the kingdom of God, and his righteousness, and all these things shall be added to you."

to walk therein: I am the Lord your God. Ye shall therefore keep my statutes, and my judgments: which if a man do, he shall live in them: I am the Lord. None of you shall approach to any that is near of kin to him, to uncover their nakedness: I am the Lord. The nakedness of thy father, or the nakedness of thy mother, shalt thou not uncover: she is thy mother; thou shalt not uncover her nakedness. The nakedness of thy father's wife shalt thou not uncover: it is thy father's nakedness. The nakedness of thy sister, the daughter of thy father, or daughter of thy mother, whether she be born at home, or born abroad, even their nakedness thou shalt not uncover. The nakedness of thy son's daughter, or of thy daughter's daughter, even their nakedness thou shalt not uncover: for theirs is thine own nakedness. The nakedness of thy father's wife's daughter, begotten of thy father, she is thy sister, thou shalt not uncover her nakedness. Thou shalt not uncover the nakedness of thy father's sister: she is thy father's near kinswoman. Thou shalt not uncover the nakedness of thy mother's sister: for she is thy mother's near kinswoman. Thou shalt not uncover the nakedness of thy father's brother, thou shalt not approach to his wife: she is thine aunt. Thou shalt not uncover the nakedness of thy daughter in law: she is thy son's wife; thou shalt not uncover her nakedness. Thou shalt not uncover the nakedness of thy brother's wife: it is thy brother's nakedness. Thou shalt not uncover the nakedness of a woman and her daughter, neither shalt thou take her son's daughter, or her daughter's daughter, to uncover her nakedness; for they are her near kinswomen: it is wickedness. Neither shalt thou take a wife to her sister, to vex her, to uncover her nakedness, beside the other in her life time. Also thou shalt not approach unto a woman to uncover her nakedness, as long as she is put apart for her uncleanness. Moreover thou shalt not lie carnally with thy neighbour's wife, to defile thyself with her. And thou shalt not let any of thy seed pass through the fire to Molech, neither shalt thou profane the name of thy God: I am the Lord. Thou shalt not lie with mankind, as with womankind: it is abomination. Neither shalt thou lie with any beast to defile thyself therewith: neither shall any woman stand before a beast to lie down thereto: it is confusion. (Leviticus 18:1–23)

As I mentioned previously, some in the organized church are embracing ungodliness in order to stay relevant, at least here in the United States. Avoid such ministries there. Have nothing to do with them unless they repent. They claim God has changed, which is impossible for Him to do; He changes not.[72] It is the steadfastness of the person of God. Since He exists in a timeless state, His virtues cannot change because He is always true to Himself.[73] I have seen how grieved the heart of the Lord is over churches that promote false doctrine and show no accountability. But the people embrace these teachings, thinking the good they do will outweigh the lies they've accepted. I'm convinced this is one of the primary reasons that we have church closures as God in His judgment comes after a season of mercy as He implores those leaders to deal righteously with their error, but too often in their rebellion they do not respond appropriately, and many suffer the consequences. It is all too common that in their error they no longer can discern the voice of God or the conviction of the Holy Spirit. Do not waste your time on these churches. Rebuke them and leave them for God to deal with.

---

[72] Malachi 3:6: "For I am the Lord, I change not; therefore, ye sons of Jacob are not consumed."

[73] Psalms 138:2: "I will worship toward thy holy temple and praise thy name for thy lovingkindness and for thy truth: for thou hast magnified thy word above all thy name."

Some of the churches, in the United States, have deteriorated to such an extent that we no longer recognize sin or the demonic influences that we attach ourselves to. We must always be aware that Jesus suffered and died to deliver us from sin, not to validate it. And yet today many of our churches have embraced sins such as homosexuality in order to remain relevant in a culture that can no longer stand to be convicted of sin and no longer has a fear of the Lord's wrath.[74] Beware of those in ministry like Jannes and Jambres, who while serving in the priesthood undermined Moses to their own destruction, for there are those in the church deceived in their thinking who are like those who promote false positions for personal gain. Beware of such people, be quick to rebuke them and even cast them out should they not accept your rebuke and repent. Remember therefore to speak the truth in love and teach holiness so that your work is not ridiculed by the Muslim whom you dwell among and thereby become a reproach against the Lord. Even so, do not adopt the culture in the spirit of the age like some in the US church have done, for the Muslim too, while proclaiming to be holy, engages in the same works, claiming Islam to be the final expression of God. The Muslims engage in slavery, lying in the name of God, jihad, kidnapping, oppression of women, rape, female genital mutilation, honor killing and forced conversion to name a few. This is not the reflection of the person of God, but these are the works of the flesh done in the spirit of Cain, for the fruit (evidence) of God's Spirit is

---

[74] 1 Timothy 3:1–9: "This know also, that in the last days perilous times shall come. For men shall be lovers of their own selves, covetous, boasters, proud, blasphemers, disobedient to parents, unthankful, unholy, Without natural affection, trucebreakers, false accusers, incontinent, fierce, despisers of those that are good, Traitors, heady, high-minded, lovers of pleasures more than lovers of God; Having a form of godliness but denying the power thereof: from such turn away. For of this sort are they which creep into houses, and lead captive silly women laden with sins, led away with divers lusts, Ever learning, and never able to come to the knowledge of the truth. Now as Jannes and Jambres withstood Moses, so do these also resist the truth: men of corrupt minds, reprobate concerning the faith. But they shall proceed no further: for their folly shall be manifest to all men, as theirs also was."

love, joy, peace, long-suffering, gentleness, goodness, faith, meekness, and temperance[75]—against such there is no law. The Muslim is in bondage to god of this world, who as in times past mixes among the people and deceives the nations in order to keep the people in servitude to the gods of this world. As I have said, theirs is a religion of hate and murder because their works are not accepted by God, no one's is. Continue to pray for them and endure hardship for their sake so that many will come to salvation through your example.

Ashtoreth (a power / *exousia*), a contemporary of Molech under Baal, is the goddess of fertility, the worship of whom embraces pornography, incest, bisexuality, homosexuality, and orgies. This spirit, together with Molech, provides a constant supply of children to be sacrificed to the gods, today primarily in the form of abortion. Our adversary hates mankind and seeks nothing less than to steal, kill, and destroy anything made in the image of God.

Molech (a power / exousia) or Moloch, one of the preeminent Canaanite gods subject to Baal, is the driving spiritual influence behind abortion. In their day, the Canaanites would beat a drum to distract the mother from hearing the cries of her dying infants.

> And thou shalt not let any of *thy seed pass through the fire to Molech*, neither shalt thou profane the name of thy God: I am the Lord. (Leviticus 18:21, emphasis added)

The word seed here connotes a pre-birth state of existence and burn them refers to a form of desecration. Today's abortion procedures often use a suction machine that makes a rhythmic sound similar to

---

[75] Galatians 5:23–25: "But the fruit of the Spirit is love, joy, peace, longsuffering, gentleness, goodness, faith, Meekness, temperance: against such there is no law. And they that are Christ's have crucified the flesh with the affections and lusts. If we live in the Spirit, let us also walk in the Spirit. Let us not be desirous of vain glory, provoking one another, envying one another."

that of a drum, and for the same reason to distract the mother from the sounds of death taken place. Ninety-five percent of abortions are performed because the pregnancy is unwanted and inconvenient with the couple trading the blessing of having children for freedom from the burden of the financial cost of raising them. In this way they prosper financially in the natural with their prayers answered by false gods. This is how both Ashtoreth and Molech create the endless cycle of death offered to Baal as Satan's primary goal, because of the latter's hatred toward God, of destroying mankind in our innocence who are made in God's image and whom our adversary believes took his inheritance as God preferred us over the angels as the recipients of His love. I fear for those who have endorsed this spirit in the church. The recent advance of abortion laws, including the intent of taking the innocent viable life of an unborn child at full term, will soon give way to a post term abortion agenda of infanticide. I fear by the time you read this that not only will legislators have legalized this but also, they will be promoting euthanasia of the infirmed and elderly here in the United States. We have most certainly come to a crossroads as a nation here in the United States as the removal of the one who restrains exposes the depravity of mankind, even in this modern age with all the advancements of a civilized society. That we could possibly regress to paganism and heathenism is almost beyond belief, especially in the church.

For example, how is it possible for believers to choose taking the life of an unborn child, which is clearly against God's will, and continue to think they are disciples of Jesus Christ? This is the spirit of Molech at work within the church. If you know anyone who has had an abortion, please know that the love of God is there to heal and

> "Sons of God" is a term used to describe fully mature believers, both male and female, as progenitors (exact representations) of our heavenly Father in the image (pattern) of Jesus Christ.

restore them. Encourage those who have committed this sin, that nothing can separate them from God's love and give them forgiveness and hope they need. During this time of the removal of restraint, should the church not engage fully on behalf of the righteous standards of scripture, I fear for it, as we will reap a terrible harvest should we not be diligent and take a stand against this modern-day genocide.

Gaia (a principality / arche) is the worship of the earth. Gaia, in the order of Greek mythology, came after the god Chaos and was considered the mother of all things: nature, harvest, animals, fertility, motherhood, birth, procreation, creation, and life. She also came before Cronus, the father of Zeus. In the hierarchy of demonic beings, Gaia manifests in the spirit of environmentalism and is the driving force behind the global warming movement, which is currently finding a new expression in the proposed green movement. This spirit withholds mankind's mandate to possess the earth for God and keeps human beings under the curse so that we cannot fulfill our destiny as the redeemed sons and daughters of God, because the earth is under a curse until the time comes of those who will be revealed in the last days as the sons of God who walk in the fullness of the image of Jesus, doing the works of Christ that He said we would do[76] but that we have not yet seen in their fullness. The planet longs also for the full redemption of mankind to relieve it from the curse in hope as it is written.

The spirit of environmentalism is being heavily promoted in the entertainment industry. The movies *Avatar* and *Guardians of the Galaxy* are prime examples of this spirit, where the concept

---

[76] Mark 16:15–18: "And he said to them, Go ye into all the world, and preach the gospel to every creature. He that believeth and is baptized shall be saved; but he that believeth not shall be damned. And these signs shall follow them that believe; In my name shall they cast out demons; they shall speak with new tongues; They shall take up serpents; and if they drink any deadly thing, it shall not hurt them; they shall lay hands on the sick, and they shall recover."

of living planets that both provide and protect us and are real and to be worshipped is the underlying influence that reinforces our Adamic nature. Christians need to avoid this mentality and not be overly immersed in environmentalism but instead understand that we are stewards of the earth. And even though creation's hope is its redemption, this will only come as we seek to mature from children into the sons and daughters of God.

> For I consider that the sufferings of this present time are not worthy to be compared with the glory that is to be revealed to us. ***For the anxious longing of the creation waits eagerly for the revealing of the sons of God. For the creation was subjected to futility, not willingly, but because of Him who subjected it, in hope that the creation itself also will be set free from its slavery to corruption into the freedom of the glory of the children of God.*** For we know that the whole creation groans and suffers the pains of childbirth together until now. And not only this, but also, we ourselves, having the first fruits of the Spirit, even we ourselves groan within ourselves, waiting eagerly for our adoption as sons, the redemption of our body. (Romans 8:18–23 NASB, emphasis added)

While we certainly need to be good stewards of the planet, we call home, we cannot continue to submit to the deception of these demonic influences promoted by weak scientific research and celebrities who all stand to profit through its proliferation. If a church is overly engaged in these activities to the detriment of the work of the church, then its congregants should be made aware, repent, and get back on track with their main focus of evangelism and discipleship, raising believers to maturity, developing their discernment, and finding the fullness of purpose God has for them after they abandon their entanglement with these forces of darkness, as God is faithful to forgive us if we but repent of our sins, even the most vile.

Greet the pastors for me especially pastor Habib Sadiq, I remember meeting him in Dubai and his passion for the ministry.

Blessings. Madson

Rulers of Darkness

IN MY PREVIOUS LETTER, Tariq, I spoke on the power of the influence of principalities and powers and discussed how the three types of cultures are used to rule mankind, along with their various forms of government to enforce their rule. Just as in God's heavenly order there are three archangels that govern over the angelic host, this trichotomy is found in the first layer of the hierarchy of the demonic realm (principalities) and the subsequent national governments and their various branches, along with military, to enforce their authority over mankind (powers). The next rank of demonic authority are the societal controls through state, local, or civil structures, education, arts and entertainment, and religious institutions. The scriptures are replete with examples of local government and religious structures as they influenced the Greek society of Jesus's day. People ascribed descriptions of these "rulers of darkness" as they saw the influence of their existence in everyday life. For example, in the third book of John, the apostle writes to the church about a man in a leadership role named Diotrephes. The scripture speaks of how even though Diotrephes is an elder in the church, he resists the apostle to the point that anyone who received John was cast out of the fellowship. One of the interesting things about this passage is his name Diotrephes, which literally means "one who is nourished by Jove," that is, Jupiter or Zeus. Here is man in church leadership who is led not by the Holy Spirit but by a demonic influence whose main purpose is to resist the furtherance of the church in this territory by rejecting apostolic reciprocity.

> "I wrote to the church: but Diotrephes, who loveth to have the preeminence among them, receiveth us not. Wherefore, if I come, I will remember his deeds which he doeth, prating against us with malicious words: and not content therewith, neither doth he himself receive the brethren, and forbiddeth them that would, and casteth them out of the church. Beloved, follow not that which is evil, but that which is good. He that doeth good is of God: but he that doeth evil hath not seen God." 3 John 1:9–11(KJV)

Do not let religious doctrine deceive you into believing that Christians are not susceptible to demonic influence. Here is a clear example in scripture of a Christian who has. Free will is the vehicle by which you submit to whatever you allow yourself to be influenced by. Therefore, claiming to be a believer does not guarantee your salvation. It is only the first step to a greater reality. Do not confuse what I'm saying as being contrary to the security of the believer, but know that throughout scripture there are many examples of those who claim to be followers of God, but their lives never produce the fruit of righteousness needed to bear witness to the claim that they were indeed known of God.[77] You are not a Christian simply because you claim to be one; you're a Christian because your life demonstrates you're a Christian (i.e., a disciple of Christ). Rulers of darkness represent the potential of the exploitation of the minds of human beings through the depravity of their thoughts, which eventually lead to acts of wickedness. Therefore, teach holiness and pay attention to the evidence of the fruit of the spirit developing among your people that may come from external influences found in society.

---

[77] Matthew 7:21: "Not every one that saith to me, Lord, Lord, shall enter into the kingdom of heaven; but he that doeth the will of my Father who is in heaven."

Spiritual Wickedness in High Places

TARIQ, I NEED TO break down this last expression of demonic control to appeal to a wider scope of understanding. Unfortunately, this is where the church has expended most of its efforts. We have divorced ourselves from the spiritual responsibility of impacting our world for God by failing to address the more dominant authorities in the demonic realm and have instead preached an incomplete message, choosing rather to focus our work on the salvation aspects of pastoralism and evangelism and thereby neglecting the apostolic, prophetic, and teaching[78] responsibilities required to fulfill the mandates of our Lord to possess or fill the earth with His glory. The term *spiritual* here refers to beings that are higher in order than mankind but inferior to God. *Wickedness* refers to mankind's potential for depravity, iniquity, and evil desires and the darkness of a sinful nature that holds sway over one's ability to live righteously of his or her own accord. Lastly, *high places* connotes the individual's mental capacity that allows him to exercise his physical and/or mental ability to reason, but that leads him to mental darkness and iniquity. The scriptures refer to this weakness to resist as being driven by the "lust of the eyes,

---

[78] 1 Corinthians 12:28: "And God hath set some in the church, first apostles, secondarily prophets, thirdly teachers, after that miracles, then gifts of healings, helps, governments, diversities of tongues."

the lust of the flesh, and the pride of life."[79] These are the demonic influences that are constantly tempting us to sin. They are what I refer to as the ground-level assault.

As much as I enjoy ministering to people, the reality is that if you overly engage in this level of warfare, you will find yourself in constant pastoral mode. You will never find the end-all to every situation because the needs of the flesh are endless. Ultimately there is a finality to the process, so rather than go through the litany of issues you will face when pastoring people, let me encourage you instead to focus your pastoral work on one main subject: sonship.

For the church to fulfill its mandates so that mankind can be free to overcome the snares of our enemies, we must focus on dethroning these demonic structures in both the heavenly realm and in the lives of each believer. This will ultimately happen once the church learns to love unconditionally the way God loves and stops judging those who have not come to salvation.[80] Ultimately we will demonstrate this to the extent the demonic hierarchy will finally understand the wisdom of God when He revealed to them that we were chosen over them, which the scripture calls "the mystery of God." I will write more about this later. For now, know this: since the removal of restraint[81] began, a spirit of covetousness has permeated global society.

---

[79] 1 John 2:15: "Love not the world, neither the things that are in the world. If any man love the world, the love of the Father is not in him. For all that is in the world, the lust of the flesh, and the lust of the eyes, and the pride of life, is not of the Father, but is of the world. And the world passeth away, and the lust thereof: but he that doeth the will of God abides forever."

[80] Ephesians 3:9–11: "And to make all men see what is the fellowship of the mystery, which from the beginning of the world hath been hid in God, who created all things by Jesus Christ: To the intent that now to the principalities and powers in heavenly places might be known by the church the manifold wisdom of God, According to the eternal purpose which he purposed in Christ Jesus our Lord."

[81] 2 Thessalonians 2:5–7: "Do you not remember that while I was still with you, I was telling you these things? And you know what restrains him now, so that in his time he will be revealed. For the mystery of lawlessness is already at work; only he who now restrains will do so until he is taken out of the way."

It began back in the 1960s and has since become a worldwide reality among the youth, propagated mainly through the education system. My observation is that principalities have influenced the minds of those in government since World War II, and the stage has been set through social engineering to position the elitist agenda against the voting populace. We saw this during the recent elections in the United States when the voting constituency rejected candidates of both parties and voted in a third-party non-politician. He successfully garnered the votes from the Republican voting constituency and is on a path to deliberately dismantle the regressive programs of recent presidents from both parties.

Since I'm on the subject, let me state that the scriptures are clear about God's plans for the earth and the destiny of mankind, which were established before creation. It is inevitable that God will need to redeem the times, and it is well established in scripture that He rarely uses those who should seem obvious or deserving, but almost always He chooses from the least of these to accomplish His will. I think it more than coincidence that the United States' new president is not affected by the need to conform to the politically correct liberal ideology that has engulfed the whole earth and that his rhetoric shows he is concerned about the needs of others since his personal successes are substantial. Mostly I am impressed that during this season when God is restoring the concept of sonship in government as he is engaging his sons and daughters as progenitors or extensions of Himself in government positions, preferring them to entrenched politicians. This is a kinglier approach to governing and is contrary to the democratic process, which does not know how to rule by decree but instead works to manipulate through rebellion and moves toward ungodliness. These things that are self-evident should

> **The pursuit of happiness is the failing desire of the soulish person, but the joy of the Lord is the promise of God for those who believe regardless of circumstances.**

be an encouragement to those who understand divine protocol; however, they will not be to those who judge after the flesh.

Our government, here in the US has undermined and stripped our education system of any sense of posterity by removing history and civics from the classroom, which has left us with an emotionally unstable population who are then easily manipulated through their soulishness by principalities through powers and rulers of darkness, and the Babylonian systems that are in place through social engineering. It's unfortunate that people do not understand how to translate celestial activity into the terrestrial but still judge using their Adamic nature, not understanding the plans and purposes of God. I write these things to you not fully knowing the details of spiritual activity in your territory but in the hope that you may, through our correspondence, find a commonality of the unfolding wisdom of God being released in this season. I also hope that you, through this knowledge, come to understand that my words are confirmed by the Holy Spirit.

These systems I am speaking of are reinforced by two subcultures, the societal class and caste systems. **Class systems** are those societies where individuals advance their status or position through their education and/or work ethic to improve themselves socially and economically. This is most prevalent in Western culture where Judeo-Christian values, freedom, free markets, and capitalism drive an entrepreneurial paradigm, where the pursuit of happiness is the societal norm, and where one is only limited by one's individual efforts.

The Caste system, on the other hand, means you're born into your station in life and have little or no hope of ever changing or improving your own or your family's well-being. This is the philosophy of most Eastern cultures. Beliefs like karma and reincarnation are a direct result of Eastern religious thought where your future is predisposed, and you're subjected to a future you have little control over. It is a fatalistic mind-set and is contrary to Western thought, where the individual has total control of her own destiny. This is another way principalities and powers seek to control us, by working these subcultures against one another. The facts of recorded history are undeniable as to which is the superior system. Just look at which countries have contributed to the advancement of civilization as we know it today. Class-based societies have outpaced and outperformed caste-based societies globally. Class-based entrepreneurial advancements have been the driving force behind societal improvements in developing countries since the expansion of the British Empire. One must ask the question, with such obvious validation of class-based economics, why there would be such continuing rejection of these facts and of reasonable thought, unless there were outside forces attempting to intervene and subvert mankind's progression toward a prosperous civilization.

In the United States, leftist, liberalism is causing a shift toward a caste-based society through the Democratic Party's efforts to deconstruct the class-based freedoms we have enjoyed so that the globalist elitist agenda will advance against the freedoms offered in God's kingdom. The deconstruction of the middle class in a country is necessary to strip away opportunity and the hope that is generated among a free people. Converting places like the United States into a caste-based culture strengthens government control where a people devoid of hope can be more easily manipulated and stripped of their wealth so that those in control of government might prosper at the expense of the people.

> **The process of time is the written legacy of mankind's journey as we struggle against forces more powerful than we are and as the Creator of the universe reveals Himself as our loving Father equipping us for the next life, where we will inherit all that He has prepared for us.**

In the past, we've seen how principalities have converged to shift the balance of control and how the forces of our adversary try to maintain their foothold on the destiny of mankind as Christianity, which has spread to become the dominant religion in the world, reveals to us that the propagation of the love of God will ultimately cause the meek to inherit the earth.[82] In past generations, we've seen that advancement of freedom and self-governance by a moral people has outperformed all other societal structures. This will continue to be the case moving forward as freedom-seeking people aspire to emulate those who have demonstrated the advantages of these truths. As we examine recent history, we see that various expressions of heteronomous cultures have all been defeated or are retreating. In recent memory, Fascism, Nazism, and Communism ultimately were defeated by freedom-loving theonomous peoples in autonomous cultures. Even communist countries such as Russia and China have had to adopt capitalism in order to advance economically.

The current heteronomous system of control is being expressed through socialism and through what has become the new face of heteronomy, "postmodernism," which is just the new terminology for the same adversary. Heteronomous culture, from Fascism to the dangers of postmodernism, doesn't believe in the individual, logic, dialogue, goodwill, facts, or the notion that human beings can govern themselves. These are all moot points, and the emphasis is on the collective, at the expense of the individual. Again, this is driven by the orphan's desire for legitimacy through associated identity politics and the instability of the emotional state of the soulish man.

In summation, all mankind is moving toward God's ultimate purpose of the restoration of all things, where He reconciles mankind unto Himself through a remnant of those who willfully, joyfully, and sincerely submit to His desire to have an intimate, authentic relationship with their Creator. For the failings of mankind is our Adamic nature, in which self-preservation drives a "provide and protect" paradigm, by which the unredeemed are also driven, being slaves to the fear found in their soul's void of the submission to the spirit of God. Ultimately the orphan mentality and fatherlessness is the root of mankind's problems. From the family to government

---

[82] Matthew 5:5: "Blessed are the meek: for they shall inherit the earth."

control, mankind wishes to be provided for with the confidence that there is something on which or someone on whom we can rely. This is what drives the liberal thinking and why most liberals reject God and the patriarchal paradigm. Their confidence is in having a King Saul rule over them and in believing that the government will replace and fulfill the role of our heavenly Father to the point of rebellion against all that is good, such as marriage, family, and faith in God. Liberals may even desire anarchy and subscribe to the belief that everyone is doing what is right in their own eyes. This culture of extreme control eventually drives the caste mentality, where the elite are empowered to the point of tyranny. But for the promise of provision and protection, the unregenerate mind willingly submits, and these people exchange the image of God for the idolatry of the things of the world, which cannot satisfy either the things of the spirit nor the desires of the soul.

The Enemy Within

BROTHER TARIQ, I'VE DONE what I can to lay some foundation of understanding of the plan and purpose of God and to expose the adversary and his hierarchy of control in the doings of mankind as he works to maintain that control and postpone God's final judgment on him and those who would follow after him. It's difficult to expose these spirits without first addressing the strongholds within God's church that may not be widely known. We need to understand that our sins often become the foothold for the hierarch of these demonic spirits to function. I will write again in more detail about what it means to be an authentic Christian, but for now understand that the effects of illegitimate and immature church structures (lack of biblical protocol and principles in the local assembly such as unbelief, mental assent [ever learning but never coming to the knowledge of the truth], timidity, compromise, grumbling, murmuring, high-mindedness, idolatry, covetousness, disobedience, subscribing to the prosperity gospel, and denial of spiritual authority, just to name a few) are the issues we must address if the church is going to advance through this season.

The Orphan mind-set (our human condition grounded in our Adamic nature), also known first as fatherlessness, is a condition wherein Satan accuses us night and day before God of our unworthiness as His children. He uses the orphan mind-set to promote condemnation and not conviction (which comes by the Holy Spirit). Satan feeds the orphan mentality with a substitute sense of security; this will continue to fuel the orphan's need for government oversight as a replacement for God the Father as a provider. (Sam Soleyn's book *My Father! My Father!* goes into great detail about the effects of fatherlessness in our relationships from our parents all the way to societal impact at various levels of interaction. This is mandatory reading material if you want to stay on the cutting edge of this topic.) Again, our Adamic orphaned operating system is the foundation of the decision-making process we are relegated to using unless we continually set our hearts to follow God's Word and His will for our lives. Christians need to devote time not only to prayer, study, and reading the scriptures but also to the implementation of biblical principles and divine protocol to aid them in overcoming their Adamic nature.

Universalism is the belief that all paths lead toward God, that all religions are the same, that there are no absolutes, and that you can create your own truth and apply it however you want in order to find God. This is a false teaching propagated through celebrity endorsements and is not compatible with the gospel of Jesus Christ. Only through the redemptive work of Christ Jesus the Messiah can one be restored to fellowship with God. If you believe there are other paths to God, then you cannot be a Christian. It is the singular absolute truth of the Christian faith. Know this, that that every religion is exclusive. If you're a Christian, then you must accept that no one gets to the Father apart from Jesus Christ. If you believe otherwise, you are not saved.

Humanism is a form of atheism where human beings control their own destiny because they believe mankind can solve its own issues apart from God and that the human spirit cannot reconcile itself to a God who allows such travesty in the world. While I understand the offense taken and why humanists feel a good God would not behave in this way, they neither understand the plans and purposes of God nor seek Him to gain that understanding. There is evil in the world, which the atheist cannot reconcile. Pray for them and believe God for their deliverance from these strongholds. I've presented a limited example of the spiritual adversaries we face, unlike the more common ones like Jezebel and Absalom etc, who are well-known by the church. I will not spend any time writing on the spiritual strongholds, already discussed by others who are well established.

Nourished by Zeus

In the Third Epistle of John, we read about a man named Diotrephes, a leader in the local church. He is an elder and does not receive the apostolic grace that is trying to come to the church. He is so adamant about it that he casts out anyone who would try to receive it. The interesting thing about him is his name. The name Diotrephes[83] means "one who is nourished by the god Jupiter (Zeus)." This man is not being led by the Holy Spirit but by a principality. As you may know, Jupiter was the chief Roman god.[84] His name means "ruler of the sky," and he had control of the weather, for example, the rain and thunder. And here is a man, a leader in the church, who is being led by this principality, and the stronghold that is present within him does not want the apostolic grace of the apostle John to come into the local body. Thereby Diotrephes is hindering the work of God through the church. The lesson here is that just because you call yourself a Christian, it does not mean you are immune to demonic influence. The strength of the church is the foundation built by apostles and prophets, which is why it is necessary that whatever you build on the earth, you must build according to

---

[83] The name Diotrephes means "nourished by Jove" (Jupiter or Zeus). He is a proud, arrogant man mentioned in 3 John 9.
[84] *The Screwtape Letters* by C. S. Lewis is a masterful book concerning the inner workings of the hierarchy of the demonic realm. Also *Pigs in the Parlor* by Frank Hammond is a great resource for understanding how to deal with the demonic in the church. I highly recommend both books.

Ephesians 4.[85] The strength of apostolic ministry is that it brings governance; it has the ability to rule over demonic influences. It is evident in 3 John 1:10 that the apostle John has every intention of doing this when he comes to Diotrephes's church. There are many in the church who believe that Christians cannot be influenced by the demonic, but this passage in 3 John proves otherwise. It is clear in the passage that the free will of mankind is subject to whatever spirit we submit ourselves to:

> I wrote unto the church: but Diotrephes, who loveth to have the preeminence among them, receiveth us not. ***Wherefore, if I come, I will remember his deeds* which he doeth, prating against us with malicious words: and not content therewith,** *neither doth he himself receive the brethren, and forbiddeth them that would, and casteth them out of the church.* Beloved, follow not that which is evil, but that which is good. He that doeth good is of God: but he that doeth evil hath not seen God. (3 John 1:9–11 KJV)

The Spirit of Unrighteous Mammon (the Prosperity Gospel)

When the children of Israel crossed into the Promised Land, they took the city of Jericho and were told *not to take of the spoils of their conquest*. A man named Achan ignored the mandate and stole some of the gold and idols for himself and hid them in his tent. This caused God to remove Himself from the battle against the city of Ai (a pile of rubble), a city with no walls. The Israelites lost the battle when they should have easily defeated their foe. Achan's sin became

---

[85] Ephesians 4:11–12: "And he gave some, apostles; and some, prophets; and some, evangelists; and some, pastors and teachers; For the perfecting of the saints, for the work of the ministry, for the edifying of the body of Christ."

a reproach for which he later died, along with his whole family, who were stoned.

The prosperity movement, which was birthed in the United States at the start of the charismatic movement, is the expression of unrighteous mammon. I have no issue with God blessing His people. God expects us to live well and represent Him, serving as an example of how He provides for those who are His especially, but this deceptive doctrine promotes the concept that God's plan is to help you gain wealth at the exclusion of all else. It was facilitated by a false prophet named Balaam who used his prophetic gift for personal gain.[86] Balaam tried repeatedly to negotiate his gift for the promise of monetary gain, and God had Balaam's own donkey speak to him because in his madness he could not see the angel who was sent to destroy him. Today many in the church have embraced this doctrine, forfeiting the work of the ministry for this form idolatry, which is also a form of Baal worship.

The apostle Peter addressed this in one of his epistles as a warning to those who would engage in this practice. It seems that the televangelists in the United States are the worst offenders, but this is a global stronghold within the church. The time of God's patience is coming to an end as these false servants have enriched themselves beyond reason, especially at the expense of the poor. There is no room for this doctrine in the apostolic church.

---

[86] Numbers 22:5–7, 22: "He sent messengers therefore unto Balaam the son of Beor to Pethor, which is by the river of the land of the children of his people, to call him, saying, Behold, there is a people come out from Egypt: behold, they cover the face of the earth, and they abide over against me: Come now therefore, I pray thee, curse me this people; for they are too mighty for me: peradventure I shall prevail, that we may smite them, and that I may drive them out of the land: for I wot that he whom thou blessest is blessed, and he whom thou cursest is cursed. *And the elders of Moab and the elders of Midian departed with the rewards of divination in their hand; and they came unto Balaam, and spake unto him the words of Balak. ... And God's anger was kindled because he went:* and the angel of the Lord stood in the way for an adversary against him. Now he was riding upon his ass, and his two servants were with him."

The Lord knoweth how to deliver the godly out of temptations, and to reserve the unjust to the day of judgment to be punished: But chiefly them that walk after the flesh in the lust of uncleanness and despise government. Presumptuous are they, self-willed, they are not afraid to speak evil of dignities. Whereas angels, which are greater in power and might, bring not railing accusation against them before the Lord. But these, as natural brute beasts, made to be taken and destroyed, speak evil of the things that they understand not; and shall utterly perish in their own corruption; ***And shall receive the reward of unrighteousness, as they that count it pleasure to riot in the day time. Spots they are and blemishes, sporting themselves with their own deceiving's while they feast with you; Having eyes full of adultery, and that cannot cease from sin; beguiling unstable souls: a heart they have exercised with covetous practices; cursed children: Which have forsaken the right way, and are gone astray, following the way of Balaam the son of Bosor, who loved the wages of unrighteousness; But was rebuked for his iniquity: the dumb ass speaking with man's voice forbad the madness of the prophet. These are wells without water, clouds that are carried with a tempest; to whom the mist of darkness is reserved for ever. For when they speak great swelling words of vanity, they allure through the lusts of the flesh, through much wantonness, those that were clean escaped from them who live in error. While they promise them liberty, they themselves are the servants of corruption: for of whom a man is overcome, of the same is he brought in bondage.*** For if after they have escaped the pollutions of the world through the knowledge of the Lord and Savior Jesus Christ, they are again entangled therein, and overcome, the latter end is worse with them than the beginning. For it had been better for them not to have known the way of righteousness, than, after they have known it, to turn from the holy commandment delivered to them. But it is happened to them according to the true proverb, the dog is turned to his own vomit again; and the sow that was washed to her wallowing in the mire. (2 Peter 2:9–22, emphasis added)

The Roman Circus and the Spirit of Entertainment

This spirit seeks to preoccupy us with things that bring us pleasure, which could be almost anything. This spirit is evident in everyday things like TV and movies, golf and football, and especially video games and the internet. Now none of these things are bad in and of themselves (I am not trying to promote some kind of legalism here). The danger of the spirit of entertainment is that it "steals" our time. We can get so caught up with things that are not very important that we don't pray, do devotions, witness at work, or minister to those hurting around us. We are no longer involved in Bible studies, let alone making adequate time for reading God's Word, and we've forgotten what it means to fellowship. We've become so busy in the United States, and we have internalized everything to the point that we no longer even know who our neighbor is. And this spirit has infiltrated the church to such an extent that when the world looks at us, we don't look any different from the world. Here in the US believers are not to be Americans first; we are supposed to be kingdom people and to offer a counterculture, a kingdom paradigm. US culture is demonized; every culture in the world is. Christians are supposed to be aliens and strangers, a peculiar people, a light set on a hill, and the salt of the earth. It has gotten so bad that we have gone so far as to make God our servant. We come to church and give God thirty minutes of worship. We spend forty-five minutes to listening to our pastor preach, and if he doesn't tell at least two jokes and a relevant story, we think the message is not anointed or, I daresay, not entertaining enough for us. Then we come to the altar and ask God to heal us, bless us, and meet our needs when we haven't done anything for Him all week, and we wonder why He's not moving in our lives. It's not because He's not willing but because we're not moving. And on top of it all, we think people who don't receive don't have any faith, so we dump condemnation upon each other. It is no wonder the world thinks the church is full of hypocrisy.

We must not become like Diotrephes and be ruled by any other spirit than the Holy Spirit. It's time we began to take our faith more seriously. When was the last time we did any real fasting? We have in a sense neglected the great salvation Jesus bought for us. God is looking for people who will give their lives for the truth. I believe that if we can come to that place, He will move heaven and earth for us. When we turn our own upside-down world right side up, He will empower us to reach the lost for Him. I'd like to come to the place Peter came to, being so full of the kingdom that I could preach to a crowd for three minutes and see three thousand people get saved. Isn't that a life worth living for, a life worth dying for?

Socialized Christianity

Socialized Christianity is a behavioral condition that manifests in many forms. Socialized Christianity affects the body on a corporate level. It can be difficult to see because it disguises itself in activities that look ministry based. It has the appearance of ministry but manifests in programs and activities that are not true ministry, things that the scriptures say have the appearance of religion but have no power. It's like clouds with no water. We go through the motions, but there's no evidence that we have accomplished anything for God. Everything becomes rhetorical, and yet somehow, we think we are serving the purposes of God even though we are bearing little or no fruit.

Now every church has common mandates—save the lost, heal the brokenhearted, and reach out to the poor. These are all good things, and we should do them. Each church should also have specific mandates that may be exclusive to it. Perhaps the church has strong apostolic grace and God has ordained it to be a governing church with a presbytery like the church in Jerusalem, or perhaps the church has a strong pioneering grace for church planting, like the church in Antioch. These things are determined by the strength of the grace that is manifested within the congregation, because the church is not a building; the people are the church. This is one of the reasons that your church's vision will change if God can raise up certain giftings or graces.

A church should find itself adapting its vision to the grace that is developing within the congregation. The vision to be a passionate, Spirit-filled, soul-winning church is what I would classify as a general vision that God wants for every church. But maybe you've birthed a more specific vision like the Antioch church. Paul, after many years of being a troublemaker[87] in the church, found himself leaving Tarsus with Barnabas, only to eventually arrive in Antioch. There he was mentored in the prophetic. The least of the prophets, he was not even called Paul during this time. After year under Barnabas's mentoring, he was then set apart by the Holy Spirit with Barnabas to begin his apostolic ministry. Before this time, the Antioch church had a prophetic ministry, but now the vision was going to change; they'd now become an apostolic sending church. The key thing to note here is that before a ministry is apostolic, it must first be prophetic and develop "prophetic sight." This prophetic grace guided Paul throughout his apostolic ministry.

Tariq, let's suppose, though, that your church has not been able to develop prophetic grace, and because you're building in a pastoral

---

[87] Acts 9:28–31: "And he was with them coming in and going out at Jerusalem. And he spake boldly in the name of the Lord Jesus and disputed against the Grecians: but they went about to slay him. Which when the brethren knew, they brought him down to Caesarea, and sent him forth to Tarsus. Then had the churches rest throughout all Judea and Galilee and Samaria and were edified; and walking in the fear of the Lord, and in the comfort of the Holy Ghost, were multiplied" (KJV).

or evangelistic paradigm like most American churches are, you're lacking prophetic sight. Don't make the mistake of thinking that because you have prophecy, words of wisdom, and knowledge, it is the same as the office of the prophet. All believers should be able to manifest varying levels of prophecy. Now we know God is calling us to greater things, but because we've not developed all our ministry graces, we plan all our growth administratively like a corporation. And we can't yet see exactly what we're supposed to do, so instead of finding that prophetic direction, we try to copy someone else's program because it worked for them. Then we find ourselves creating activities and programs because we've not developed our prophetic sight. A sure sign of this is that we manage everything with book-oriented teaching because it's too risky to allow people to develop their grace, and we don't have the time to mentor them because we have created a pastoral structure that constantly demands our attention, so therefore God is not honoring our efforts with accompanying signs. As a result, we find ourselves trying new things because everything we do fails to produce a breakthrough or have lasting fruit.

The answer to this problem is that we have to become an Elijah for the Elisha's in our lives, because God never used anyone from the school of the prophets. And every time God tries to raise up a prophet, there are so many strongholds in the church that a Diotrephes[88] rises up and cuts them off. Or else there is no Barnabas (son of encouragement) present to mentor the person through his or her trials. (Believe me, anyone whom God is shaping into a vessel of honor is going through a refiner's fire.) But we're too busy to form any deep meaningful relationships, and the ministry is barely manageable because, instead of building a fivefold ministry, we have built "pastoral pyramids" to handle the workload. Because of this, we find ourselves with immature and illegitimate church structures, full of activity but no real ministry. We're looking into a glass darkly[89] for

---

[88] The name Diotrephes means "nourished by Jupiter/Zeus."

[89] 1 Corinthians 13:10–12: "But when that which is *perfect* [*teleios*, "mature, lacking nothing"] is come, then that which is in part shall be done away. When I was a child, I spake as a child, I understood as a child, I thought as a

something we know is there, but we can't quite make it out because we are still immature in the ways of the Lord and have not accurately developed divine protocol—so what we do is appoint another pastor. But because we are the children of our heavenly Father, and because of His great love for us, He moves on our behalf just enough that we know He is still here. But instead of examining the ninety-nine percent of what is not working, we try to "manufacture" the one percent into something we can use to validate who we are, which leads us to the next principal spirit.

Performance-Based Spirituality

We are all looking for some kind of validation in life; we all want to hear, "Well done, good and faithful servant." It is only natural to want acceptance. That desire can lead us to performance-based spirituality, which might be also described as "works-based Christianity." This is also a *kosmokrator-skotos* (ruler of darkness) spirit; it works within the soulish areas of the believer. A clear sign of this spirit is people who are always trying to draw attention to themselves for the wrong reasons. Some of the more obvious examples are people in the worship ministry whose worship is more like a performance. Because they crave attention, they don't lead the people in praise, worship and adoration. Instead they draw attention to themselves and steal God's glory. Sometimes these worship leaders use worship to manipulate the congregation, maybe to help increase the offering. Or perhaps certain songs may be used to create an emotional state to promote an agenda. I am always listening to see if praise and worship is geared toward the soulish arena, or if the worship seems to be geared toward influencing people's emotions. One of the true signs of performance-based spirituality is what I

---

child: but when I became a man, I put away childish things. For now we see through a glass, darkly; but then face-to-face: now I know in part; but then shall I know even as also I am known."

call "Sunday morning Christians," people who smile at you, act polite, and say they love you fifty-two times a year, but you never hear from them otherwise, and they keep you at arm's length. You see this more in large churches because it's easy to come get fed and never have to get involved. But because we have numbers, we think we're making an impact. Ask yourself this: if your church closed its doors, would anyone in the community even notice? The opposite can be just as bad, people forming social cliques, which happens at the congregational level too. I think the worst form of this comes in the shape of denominationalism. Whether it's big or small, it is still "division in God's house," so beware of this.

One of the signs of a true apostolic church is its strength in relationships, people locked arm in arm in the purposes of God and their love for one another. The scripture says that five can put one hundred to flight but that one hundred will chase[90] ten thousand. Apostolic churches know how to use the "power of agreement," and because of this they have organic growth. So, as your ministry grows, focus on authentic relationships with the pastors.

I have noticed that whenever people come into covenant, it draws the Antichrist spirit. The enemy knows all too well that if the church were ever to come together in unity, his days would be numbered. One of the strengths of apostolic governance is that people fall in line; there are no agendas. Once the prophetic direction is set, it seems to galvanize everyone into one purpose. This is the grace of the apostle.

The thing about dealing with ruling spirits is that you cannot deal with them on an individual basis alone. If you do not deal with them by exposing them congregationally, you will spend an enormous amount of time and effort trying to do damage control or ignoring them and hoping the problem will go away. The last

---

[90] Leviticus 26:7–9: "And ye shall chase your enemies, and they shall fall before you by the sword. And five of you shall chase an hundred, and an hundred of you shall put ten thousand to flight: and your enemies shall fall before you by the sword. For I will have respect unto you, and make you fruitful, and multiply you, and establish my covenant with you."

thing these spirits want is to be brought out into the light, but many pastors would rather coexist with these spirits than fight this kind of battle. And because such pastors lack apostolic governance, they struggle. These spirits will increasingly manifest through people simply because they know that people don't know how to deal with them. This is where apostolic grace is needed. I believe God will hold us responsible if we allow a permissive spirit into our midst. This cavalier behavior, if not dealt with, could eventually lead to a carnival atmosphere. This is exactly what happens in most revivals, and it can kill a genuine move of the Spirit of God.

Vanity is another form of performance. We call it "victorious living" where we pretend that the problems in our lives don't exist. We suppress, medicate, and cope with our problems to keep up appearances, and eventually we become disillusioned because we are living a lie. We need to live in real breakthrough and stop pretending we are something we're not. We must become more transparent and vulnerable and stop calling ourselves Christians, yet not living like it.[91]

The Spirit of Paternalism

Paternalism or (pastor worship) is one of the biggest problems facing the church today. People are deceived into the mind-set that the pastor will do everything, and because pastors by nature are geared to serve, they are happy to oblige. So they build "pastoral pyramids" to maintain a growing but immature congregation. Here again is the need for apostolic governance. One of the sure signs of this is that the pastor is always being elevated and praised by those around him or her. The ministry of the Holy Spirit is to draw attention to Jesus and give Him the glory, not to constantly praise the pastor. Building a functioning ministry is not about the vision of the pastor; vision or "prophetic sight" is important, but a functioning

---

[91] Exodus 20:7: "Thou shalt not take the name of the Lord thy God in vain; for the Lord will not hold him guiltless that taketh his name in vain" (KJV).

ministry is about equipping the saints for the work and promoting the purposes of God in the territory God has given us. Another sure sign of this is that churches are not able to raise up their own ministry leaders. They have to constantly look outside the congregation for them, simply because they are not able to equip the members of the local congregation.

In the nineteenth chapter of Exodus, we read the story of how God called the congregation to Mount Sinai to meet with the people. They were supposed to purify themselves for three days, after which the Lord would appear to them. So terrified were they that they declared to Moses, "You speak to God for us, and we will listen. Only we don't want to hear from God, or we will die."[92] In doing so, they put their accountability on the man of God and did not want to deal with the consequences of a relationship with God. The result was that they fell into a state of idolatry. Eventually God destroyed those responsible because they had no fear or reverence for Him.

The problem today is that whenever God tries to raise up a gift or grace in the local church, these spirits, having a foothold, rise up against that person. Then one of several things happens: First, the pastor gives in to the spirit to keep the peace, in which case he or she loses the potential benefit of the grace manifesting through these people, and the church does not move to the next level. Second, the person stifles the gift that is being birthed even though God is trying to make room for it. Third, the person leaves the church because he or she has outgrown it. Fourth, those who oppose the person leave. Either way, the Holy Spirit is no longer building God's house, and the church lives in a perpetual state of postponement. Therefore, take time to recognize and support those whom the Lord is developing so that not only is the church properly built on the grace of apostles and prophets but also you have teachers, evangelists, and pastors who

---

[92] Exodus 20:18: "Now all the people witnessed the thundering's, the lightning flashes, the sound of the trumpet, and the mountain smoking; and when the people saw it, they trembled and stood afar off. Then they said to Moses, 'You speak with us, and we will hear; but let not God speak with us, lest we die'" (NKJV).

can handle congregational growth in a healthy way. The danger for you, Tariq, is that while you're coming into your apostolic role, your evangelistic grace needs to diminish so that others can grow in that area. This way you may stay focused on your apostleship. Otherwise you deny the body the benefits of the grace that's coming to you, especially the prophetic grace. I noticed you do not have many who can prophesy or declare the Word of the Lord. Place more emphasis on these two things and pray that the Lord strengthen you in both the apostolic and prophetic paradigms.

Tariq, these are just some of the spiritual strongholds that face us as we struggle in this fallen state. In this time of the removal of restraint, the exposure of the works of our adversary has created a global climate of unrest that is unprecedented in human history, and mankind must decide whom we will serve. God is looking to His people to herald the truth of His voice in this generation. The charismatic church, like Joshua, has not completed its assignment and, like Joshua, finds itself wandering aimlessly with no finish mentality. And like Joshua when he lost his mandate, the current expression of the church must declare a yieldedness to the next generation. Joshua said that he and his house would serve the Lord even though his mandate was given to Judah under the leadership of Caleb. We must not be like Ephraim and how they treated Judah once they took the mantle of leadership and become obstructionists to the new season that has come upon

> The fullness of the measure of Christ is not an expectation of our ability to do everything that Jesus could, but to do it at least according to the measure of grace we have been individually imparted. For Jesus has the Holy Spirit without measure, but we have the Holy Spirit in measure. Therefore, as we come together, we form the fullness of the body of Christ.

us by God's design because we did not complete our season in the time we had (you can read about this in the book of Hosea). We must not be like the Catholic who fights the Protestant who fights the Pentecostal who rejects the Charismatic, which in their season were all authentic expression of the church even with their failings. The church again has come to a point of reformation in which we must find a commonality of belief and in which the church of Jesus Christ must become more united.[93]

There are many immature and illegitimate ministries claiming to be the church of Jesus Christ but showing little evidence of it. The church is in need of a reformation that will bear fruit (evidence). The time of God's forbearance is diminishing as He aligns all things for the culmination of His plans. The globalist agenda is attractive to the masses primarily because mankind is a social being; like sheep, we tend to desire community as a form of security. This is attractive to the orphan's way of thinking since it seeks validation above all else. The declaration of the glory of God filling the whole earth is already carved into the future; it will happen. The question is, who will be among those who did their part in their season and in their lifetime, and were these people able to leave their complacency and see the

---

[93] Ephesians 4:7–16: "But to every one of us is given grace according to the measure of the gift of Christ. Wherefore he saith, when he ascended up on high, he led captivity captive, and gave gifts to men. (Now that he ascended, what is it but that he also descended first into the lower parts of the earth? He that descended is the same also that ascended up far above all heavens, that he might fill all things.) *And he gave some, apostles; and some, prophets; and some, evangelists; and some, pastors and teachers; For the perfecting of the saints, for the work of the ministry, for the edifying of the body of Christ: Till we all come in the unity of the faith, and of the knowledge of the Son of God, to a perfect man, to the measure of the stature of the fulness of Christ:* That we henceforth be no more children, tossed to and fro, and carried about with every wind of doctrine, by the sleight of men, and cunning craftiness, whereby they lie in wait to deceive; But speaking the truth in love, may grow up into him in all things, which is the head, even Christ: From whom the whole body fitly joined together and compacted by that which every joint supplieth, according to the effectual working in the measure of every part, maketh increase of the body to the edifying of itself in love" (emphasis added).

plan of God facilitated in its fullness? Conversely, who were those who sat on the sidelines while others carried their crosses to fulfill their destiny? Will we in our anemia do nothing and stand by while others stand by and hear, "Well done, good and faithful servants"?

Let me encourage you. God does not ask us to do more than we're able, but in our weaknesses His strength is made manifest when we but believe and engage. I can personally attest to this as I have experienced many miracles, signs, and wonders during my season of global ministry. We both witnessed during my time with you the many deliverances that took place during the teaching session on the first day of our meetings.

Tariq, I know some of my references will not directly apply to your situation, but I thought it good to speak in general of the insights we have, knowing that there will be some application for you in Pakistan and beyond. However, since people look to the example of the United States, I have used it as my main reference. My prayer is that the church in Pakistan does not fall prey to many of the errors current expressed by the US church model. Continue laboring among your brethren as a craftsman of words, knowing that God has appointed you as a minister to the people also, which I know is of little comfort since warfare with religious devils is a difficult assignment at best. But as He did with Jeremiah, God will keep and protect you, for He has known you from before you were born. As to the worldliness that has crept into the church, just know that God will use you to overcome it, so that the people will know a season of the increase of God's presence.

Greet the pastors and all those who labor among you. Hopefully the Lord will make a way for me to return to you soon and continue to impart some spiritual grace toward you.

Blessings. Madson

This Present Reality

BROTHER TARIQ, AS I mentioned in my previous letters, the works of the enemy are measurable if you know what to look for. We should first examine ourselves and prayerfully seek the Lord to discover if we are serving Him acceptably in the light of the sacrifice He made in love, having given His Son Jesus as a recompense for our fallen condition, and then we must develop a lifestyle that reflects an acceptable return to Him for all that He's done for us. It is not enough to simply be saved. We were bought with a price,[94] and we must therefore serve God acceptably however we were called, yet by His Spirit and not by the religion of men, but unto the measure of the fullness of Christ in us. We must not be like the Israelites, who mixed their devotions and did not follow God wholeheartedly. Therefore He left some of the peoples that they were supposed to conquer in the land to see if Israel would keep His ordinances.[95] Today the church,

---

[94] 1 Corinthians 7:21–24: "Art thou called being a servant? care not for it: but if thou mayest be made free, use it rather. For he that is called in the Lord, being a servant, is the Lord's freeman: likewise also he that is called, being free, is Christ's servant. Ye are bought with a price; be not ye the servants of men. Brethren, let every man, wherein he is called, therein abide with God."

[95] Judges 2:20–23: "And the anger of the Lord was hot against Israel; and he said, Because that this people hath transgressed my covenant which I commanded their fathers, and have not hearkened unto my voice; I also will not henceforth drive out any from before them of the nations which Joshua left when he died: That through them I may prove Israel, whether they will

like the Israelites, has not wholeheartedly followed God, and the removal of the one who restrains presents the opportunity for the church to come out of its introverted posture and be the expression of Jesus Christ to a lost and dying world. The church is the only global form of governance that can successfully accomplish this task because it is already present in every nation and could accomplish its mandate if it would only come to the unity of the faith.

At this time of the removal of restraint, do not look to the moves of the past for revivals and tent meetings, the previous seasons when we experienced His presence but produced no lasting, sustainable fruit, which is the hope of some, but rather look for the coming movement of God, which will be demonstrated by believers who will walk in the measure of the corporate Christ to accomplish this. For this to happen, we must fulfill the protocol in Ephesians 4[96] and the protocol of the multiple faces of grace[97] that Peter mentions in that the church must have apostolic governance and prophetic sight,

---

keep the way of the Lord to walk therein, as their fathers did keep it, or not. Therefore the Lord left those nations, without driving them out hastily; neither delivered he them into the hand of Joshua."

[96] Ephesians 4:11–16: "And he gave some, apostles; and some, prophets; and some, evangelists; and some, pastors and teachers; For the perfecting of the saints, for the work of the ministry, for the edifying of the body of Christ: Till we all come in the unity of the faith, and of the knowledge of the Son of God, to a perfect man, to the measure of the stature of the fulness of Christ: That we henceforth be no more children, tossed to and fro, and carried about with every wind of doctrine, by the sleight of men, and cunning craftiness, whereby they lie in wait to deceive; But speaking the truth in love, may grow up into him in all things, which is the head, even Christ: From whom the whole body fitly joined together and compacted by that which every joint supplieth, according to the effectual working in the measure of every part, maketh increase of the body to the edifying of itself in love."

[97] 1 Peter 4:10–11: "As every man hath received the gift, even so minister the same one to another, as good stewards of the manifold grace of God. If any man speak, let him speak as the oracles of God; if any man minister, let him do it as of the ability which God giveth: that God in all things may be glorified through Jesus Christ, to whom be praise and dominion for ever and ever. Amen."

taking us back to discipleship and teaching as our primary focus, for the evangelical model alone is insufficient to healthy growth, just as it is written in Ephesians 4:13. In other words, all five graces are necessary for the church to reach its goal of unity and helping believers to conform to the example of Jesus. And you cannot rely on just the pastoral and evangelical graces. You must have apostolic governance, prophetic sight, and teachers who can be relevant and can discern the times and the season we're in as it is written in 1 Corinthians 12:27–28:

> Now ye are the body of Christ, and members in particular. And God hath set some in the church, first apostles, secondarily prophets, thirdly teachers, after that miracles, then gifts of healings, helps, governments, diversities of tongues.

We need to recognize and help develop these graces within the church if we are to experience miracles, healings, help, governance, etc. Therefore, as you build alliances in your city and country, look for those who are like-minded in both spirit and expression of their ministry, and focus on discipleship, especially on the subject of sonship. And be aware of the advances of the adversary within the church. In the United States we've been deceived into thinking that one is either a liberal or a conservative, either a Republican or a Democrat, and believers have missed the reality of the third option for which they are responsible, that is, the kingdom of God is the kingdom of righteousness or right living, and our responsibility is to the standards of scripture and not to the ways of this world—and the church in its apprehension of the liberties found in God's grace has lost its sense of consecration and holiness and has forgotten the cross of Christ. Believers have sought easy believeism and have forgotten concepts like duty and oneness with Him, forsaking the teaching of the scriptures. But be of good cheer, for we are witnesses to your faith and good works, your devotion to the teaching of the Word, and your evangelism and much prayer. Do not overly focus on intercession as we have known it, but use specific prayers and be more task focused on the pulling down of strongholds so that you may experience breakthroughs.

Greet the congregation for me and especially the family, I pray these letters are a benefit to you. I know they're a poor substitute for being there in person, so pray that the Lord will make a way for me to come to you again soon.

Blessings, Madson

Population Control

Of the more noticeable cultural shifts taking place, population control seems to be preeminent among them as principalities realign themselves for control of mankind. As I mentioned previously, principalities are the primary instigators of cultural shifts, violent conflicts, and the wars that are taking place throughout the nations. Even though we are living in a day where the proliferation of wars and human suffering is at an all-time low, it is naive to think we are beyond the point of returning to major global conflicts. World leaders must remain diligent in the defense of peace. The push for globalization is causing massive shifts in immigration as Western culture has moved toward smaller family units and improved quality of life. The resulting decline in population has created the need for an influx of migrants to maintain their infrastructures. This is bad news for Europe, as the need for manpower has been met by a nonconforming Islamist culture from the Middle East and Africa which still advocates large families in spite of their poverty and is more prone to socialist political and religious control. Those who migrate to the United States are mostly Catholics from Mexico and South America who are very compatible with US culture and who add to its general well-being. The immigration into the USA has been and will continue to benefit the United States and aid its growth toward a more prosperous nation. The problem in the United States is that political leaders, mostly from the Democratic Party, have promoted abortion and birth control, which is the primary culprit of the declining population of the United States. They have decimated their black population through government subsidies of welfare, promoting fatherlessness and abortion to the point that black children are being aborted at higher numbers than their birth numbers. This is one of the greatest tragedies of our time and in United States history. However, as the Western practice of having smaller families continues to gain acceptance in developing countries, we will eventually have a new problem. The reversal of global population growth will leave us with a population shortfall in the next fifty to seventy-five years as the global population levels off near eleven billion and then begins to decline. We may no longer be able to maintain the infrastructure of our cities. This answer to this shortfall, which may be difficult to comprehend, is to partially replace human beings with the advancement of AI (artificial intelligence) robotics, self-driving cars and trucks, and the "Internet of Things."

Poorly taught eschatology (the study of the end times) within the church, based on illegitimate and antiquated spiritual postures, will convince many that these advancements are not to be embraced by Christians and are not of God. This mindset will keep the church from advancing if it fails to embrace these new technologies, not understanding that these new advancements, like currency, are amoral. Therefore, Christians can embrace these coming advancements as long as they operate them within a kingdom paradigm.

The soon-coming challenge of established abortion laws will be the primary catalyst of the redemption of

> **As Christians we owe our allegiances to the standard of scripture, of a God who does not change. Therefore, we surrender our rights to our opinions and submit to the principles of the kingdom of righteousness.**

the United States as God begins to judge the nations and measure their value by their acts. The removal of restraint is the final step of the three-stranded cord, which includes the proliferation of lawlessness (the nations' abandonment of scriptural morality) and the global apostasy, all of which have come to pass relatively unnoticed because God has veiled our eyes as the acceleration of His redemptive plan has already begun. The church's repositioning itself as the mountain of the Lord's house that will rest upon all the other mountains (governments) of the earth.[98] The timeline of this is still unclear, but the final sign will be the mature church operating in the ministry of Jesus Christ in its fullness, which until recently has only been revealed in a limited way because the church is still operating in its gifted stage and has not fully put away its immaturities.[99] Therefore, the corporate church has not received its fullness to operate at its full capacity. However, that day is approaching.

One of the great deceptions of our generation in the United States is that we've been told that we are either conservative or liberal, Republicans or Democrats. The truth is that these are immature positions with both strengths and weaknesses. The conservative

---

[98] Isaiah 2:2–5: "And it shall come to pass in the last days, that the mountain of the Lord's house shall be established in the top of the mountains, and shall be exalted above the hills; and all nations shall flow unto it. And many people shall go and say, Come ye, and let us go up to the mountain of the Lord, to the house of the God of Jacob; and he will teach us f his ways, and we will walk in his paths: for out of Zion shall go forth the law, and the word of the Lord from Jerusalem. And he shall judge among the nations and shall rebuke many people: and they shall beat their swords into plowshares, and their spears into pruninghooks: nation shall not lift up sword against nation, neither shall they learn war any more. O house of Jacob, come ye, and let us walk in the light of the Lord."

[99] 1 Corinthians 13:9: "For we know in part and we prophesy in part; but when the perfect comes, the partial will be done away. When I was a child, I used to speak like a child, think like a child, reason like a child; when I became a man, I did away with childish things. For now we see in a mirror dimly, but then face to face; now I know in part, but then I will know fully just as I also have been fully known. But now faith, hope, love, abide these three; but the greatest of these is love."

bases their position on facts but offers little in the way of solutions. We hear the constant clamoring of talk show pundits who revel in being factually correct but are typically nothing more than political bullies berating those who disagree and offering little in the way of solutions. The liberal, on the other hand, operates from emotionally charged soulishness, and their solutions to issues are usually worse than the problems they claim to defend. Christians often find themselves split between these two camps and forget that they are to be citizens of God's kingdom of righteousness (or right living) and that their allegiance is to the standard of scripture of a God who does not change.[100] Therefore, we surrender our rights to our opinions and submit to the principles found in scripture and of the coming kingdom of God. Jesus said that if we are truly His disciples, then we will keep His teachings, which include the entirety of both the Old Testament and the New Testament since He is the Word and the author of all scripture. It is not the believer's prerogative to pick and choose what to accept as truth. To do so is to make God conform to your image of Him, making yourself God, and therefore you blaspheme the person of God. We must never forget that Jesus suffered and died not to validate our sins but to deliver us from our sins. To live otherwise is to live in hypocrisy and to fall short of the reality of the glory God intended for us as His children.

In the United States the Democratic Party has fully embraced this ideology of heteronomous control and being deceived, have deliberately sought the destruction of our autonomous culture of freedom as they continue to establish laws that favor their platform of control over the two-party system, which was designed to keep balance by empowering the voters. They prey upon the orphan mind-set through identity politics to manipulate the population. Conservatives in their dogmatic thinking actually entertain the insanity as if they knew the truth, but as I said before, they rely on

---

[100] Malachi 3:6–8: "For I am the Lord, I change not; therefore, ye sons of Jacob are not consumed. Even from the days of your fathers ye are gone away from mine ordinances and have not kept them. Return unto me, and I will return unto you, saith the Lord of hosts. But ye said, wherein shall we return?"

facts, understanding little of truth or the ways of God. Righteous living come from the principles found in scripture.

Identity Politics is the recruitment tool of the adversary. The goal is to single out those who are marginalized from the voting populace and give them a sense of inclusion by banding them together under the banner of victimhood within the Democratic Party, which is trying to maintain strength through numbers in their opposition to God's kingdom of righteousness as it empowers the need for acceptance of the orphan mind-set that drives the self-preservation efforts of our soul. Our longing for oversight is embraced within the destructive politics of the leftist, liberal ideology of the postmodernist movement. It uses collective affiliation under the Democratic Party, which rejects the sovereignty of God as a provider in exchange for government control. This costs the individual the ability to exercise her free will. For the sake of the collective, this is the foundational basis for communist rule. It stands in direct opposition to the government of God, which is designed to provide for the disenfranchised through the love of God. It the deception of the enemy to claim that there is a substitute for the love of God through the redemptive power of the cross of Jesus Christ. It is an act of desperation as the need to increase the ranks in order to promote the liberal agenda, which in turn has fostered the need for uncommon alliances as the new collective can no longer hide itself or its declining hold on the mainstream common sense of reasonable thinking people.

Therefore, the voters have an opportunity to choose between parties, but this is being replaced in places in the United States like California with a single system of manipulation as voters must choose between the two highest-performing candidates even if they are from the same party. This is another reason the Democrats want illegal immigration and wish to allow noncitizens to vote. They continue with a policy of government overreach by promising false prosperity, which feeds the spirit of covetousness that has permeated the culture here. And this is why the Democrats now embrace Islam within their ranks, seeing as it is another form of heteronomous control they can use. They see how places like Saudi Arabia model the culture of control through religion and how the government controls the population and natural resources, thereby enriching the elites but keeping the rest of society under control. Once the natural resources of the Middle East are diminished, they will lose their appeal as their economies faulter. The Democrats are desirous of this here in the United States because they seek personal wealth above all else and at the expense of others.

Beware of these things in your territory. The reverse is happening as God is moving to free people from these heteronomous systems, and the Muslim is being reached directly by acts of the Holy Spirit through dreams and visions that will continue to manifest. We are witnesses of the love of God for the sons of the disobedience of Abraham are great, and through your efforts many will come to the knowledge of the salvation and the freedom offered by the autonomous culture they desire that Islam cannot provide. It is built into mankind's DNA to be free of the Adamic sense of self-preservation in exchange for the right to exercise the free will we were originally created with, along with the truth of why the meek will inherit the earth.

One of the many blessings of the gospel is that we as the body of Christ have a unity as part of the family of God as brothers and sisters. There is no male or female, and no color or race, when it comes to being a progenitor of our heavenly Father because we are all one family. Therefore, let no strife or hatred come between you over these issues, but choose instead to love because the love one has for another is a great witness to those who struggle to believe and will be the overcoming attribute of the people of God.

Race

As Christians, we believe that the ethnicity of a person is sacred. It is not a choice. You were born with it. Therefore, racism in the family of God is illegal, and if your church is not open to integration of peoples of varying colors, then you have a problem with your heavenly Father that needs addressing, as the love of the Father toward His children makes all believers accepted in His sight.

Marriage

Marriage is also something sacred and is the only institution that reflects all four types of love: agape, which is God's love, socially and morally; phileo, which is friendship or brotherly love; storgee, which is protective or parental love; and arous, which is romantic love, the distinct relationship between a man and a woman in the singular commitment of the marriage vow. When you say yes to the beauty of a consummate relationship, you say no to all others. If you remove agape (God's love), then you no longer have an authentic Arous (intimate romantic love). Doing whatever you want to do is how romantic love is defined nowadays, and this defiles the sacredness of romantic love. There are no boundaries with this mentality. Anything you define as worldly love is acceptable but know that it will fall short of God's purpose and will be a perversion of His intended outcome.

> Marriage is the distinct relationship between a man and a woman in the singular commitment of the marriage vow. When you say yes to the beauty of a consummate relationship, you say no to the exclusion of all others.
> Ravi Zacharias

Sexual preference is not something you were born with. It is an individual's choice. The Christian believes that the marriage bed is sacred, and that sexuality is sacred. Therefore, some people believe race is sacred but will desacralize sexuality. Marriage, from the Christians position, is the most sacred institution one can enter into; it is the reflection of God's desire toward us. We are the bride of

Christ, and the intimacy He desires with us cannot be substituted; it is in our view an absolute. but at the same time Christians are commanded to love. The responsibility of Christians is to love and never to hate. Only God can change the heart of a person, and when we love a person in spite of our differences (no matter how vile), our hope is that the love of God reflected in us will draw that person to Jesus Christ and he or she will forsake his or her sin. Therefore, as Christians in a pluralistic society, let us be both salt and light to a lost and dying world and not make the same mistake the Jews made when God chose us over them, thinking they were better, for all have sinned! Christians have to learn to love others, even those whose lifestyle is different from ours. It is in this way, by our compassion for them, that we can help them to overcome the sin in their lives. Homosexuality, however, is a choice; God has given mankind the most valuable gift in the prerogative of choice. However, God does not give you prerogative of the outcome of your choice. Our consequences are bound to our choices. Jesus did not suffer and die to validate your sin but to deliver you from your sin. People engaged in the LGBT lifestyles ultimately suffer because of the choices they've made, to the extent you not only are expected to accept the lifestyle choice but are pressed to "like the people in Sodom and Gomorrah" engage in their sin. Which is why once you give it a place of normalcy, it's never enough. The desire for acceptance and inclusion is driven by insecurity. This why it is all the more important that we both engage the conversation in love but without compromise to Gods biblical truths.

> **Christians have to better learn how to love others, even those whose lifestyle is different from ours. It is in this way, by our compassion for them, that we can help them to overcome the bondage of sin in their lives.**
> **Ravi Zacharias**

When Cain's offering was rejected, it was because his lifestyle did not measure up to the offering he presented. And what did the Lord tell him? "If you do what is right, will you not be accepted?" But if not, then sin (anything that separates you from God) is waiting at the door, and its desire is to have you, thereby keeping you separated from God. In the case of marriage, any departure from the biblical standard has severe consequences. One of the things I have learned while traveling the nations is that fact and truth are not always the same thing. You may be deathly ill (fact), but the truth is that by His stripes you can be made whole. But knowing this fact is not enough if you can't manifest a breakthrough for the one who is suffering, but because you are a child of the kingdom but not a mature son (a qualified progenitor). The kingdom you represent must not be in word only but in power. I remember on many occasions when ministering, I would be speaking as the Spirit was leading me, and I'd come to places where it seemed like I had hit a wall. I realized I had a responsibility to press through and that God's intentions might not materialize if I let unbelief overcome me in the moment.

It is the work of the adversary to hinder you at every opportunity. Walking in the confidence of who you are in Him is necessary, but often this is something that is developed over time—and unfortunately it may come with some trial and error. The greatest asset I had during my growth stage was spiritual fathers, men who sowed the seeds of experience and made themselves available to mentor me. They sowed the seeds of understanding and of the wisdom of God, which I hope I have communicated in some small way in my letters. It is an invaluable resource to have men of God help accelerate your spiritual growth. I was fortunate to have several such mentors for whom I will be forever grateful. In the natural, men birth their children, but in the spiritual sons choose their fathers. Look for men such as these and surround yourself with them. Ultimately every earthly father will direct you to a deeper relationship with our heavenly Father and the Lord Jesus. I am also grateful for those I call my brothers. We encourage one another as we walk similar paths toward God's destiny for us. Seek out such men and refuse not those who ask for your guidance as long as they follow the ways of righteousness. Avoid those who walk in rebellion and cannot take strong counsel. They will waste your time and resources.

The mandate to fulfill our destiny is tied directly to our efforts in accurately walking our path. It is said that it's like going to a university. Your parents can prepare a way and provide the finances, but if you don't apply yourself and learn, then you will not receive the degree that states you're qualified, even though others have labored for you to invest in your future. Each of us must do our part, so encourage your youth to develop their character in the things of God and not in the things of this world, or else they will be found lacking and may miss the destiny that God has provided for them.

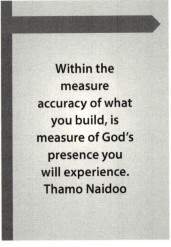

**Within the measure accuracy of what you build, is measure of God's presence you will experience.
Thamo Naidoo**

Tariq, there are many other instructions I would like to leave you with, but some instruction is necessary to be done in person because impartation is limited through these informal communications. It is the way of the kingdom. Let me know how the churches respond to the conference you're wanting to hold. I think perhaps after the rainy season next year would be a favorable time for me to come. In the meantime, let me leave you with this: The reality of the present time is that the church must get back to the foundations outlined in scripture if we are to fulfill the desires of God for our generation. In that Jesus suffered, died, and rose again, and in that we owe God a debt, our salvation was bought with a price; therefore, we must live a life that honestly reflects His sacrifice on a daily basis, and we must acknowledge that we are here to live for Him, not for Him to serve us. Know this, within the measure of accuracy of what you build is the measure of the presence of God you will experience. If we do not pattern ourselves after the example of Jesus set for us and set our goals to become more like Him, then we are neither His children nor His sons.

In this season, I see the church growing toward unity daily, but we must know that a kiaros (an open season that finishes when we complete its mandates) has no appointed time of completion. Whatever you build must cause the church to rise to its full potential, and should God grace us with a season of renewal, then the advancement will accelerate. If the church continues in its mediocre expression of the kingdom, there will continue to be a vacuum that the ungodly will fill. A great book on how the church should respond in its ability to overcome is Rick Scarborough's *Enough Is Enough*, which is a clarion call to believers to actively take their cities for God by infiltrating the Babylonian structures by which the prince of this world controls the nations. It also discusses how the people of God can advance His purposes in love to a lost and dying world by getting involved in the political processes in their communities. With less than 20% of the US population voting in the national elections that choose our president and representatives and an estimated 75% of the population identifying as Christians, Christians could easily change the outcome of the direction of the United States if we would only participate in the election process and vote our consciences. And on the state and local level if we would place our people in civic positions from our school boards to the governorships.

I pray the seriousness of my letters has encouraged you and does not seem overbearing, which is certainly not my intent. Therefore, be of good cheer, knowing that the hope we share in our future is assured in that the teaching, insights, and revelations are for your increase in the knowledge of Him and knowing, through the renewing of our minds, that the revelation of what is currently being released in the atmosphere from the throne of God is for those who have an ear to hear. Pray for those who are struggling to move from outdated spiritual postures that were relevant in another season but that have been memorialized to the point that they are now the stronghold that holds them back from the new season we are in. But understand also that the grace of God that was once wide is being narrowed so that it bears witness to those who are struggling to move forward toward their perfection[101] (*teleios*: "mature, lacking nothing"). It is God's witness that their paradigms are shifting to the newness of God's ever-increasing glory that is being revealed.

Tariq, the reality of the present time we live in is one of sobering consequence. The church has been created not only to carry God's standard to all of mankind but also to reveal His wisdom to the kingdom of darkness.[102] If we recognize that the fulfillment discussed in 2 Thessalonians 2 is the time in which we now find ourselves, then this generation of believers is responsible for a great many things, and a global paradigm shift in the body of Christ is not only inevitable but also has been in process for some time now. However, my concern is that if the current expression of the church does not rise to the occasion, then I fear we will find ourselves living in postponement until another generation develops the maturity necessary to accomplish His mandates. However, I am believing for better things not only because of brothers like you but also because in places like the United States, we are also making progress. The apostolic grace being released is gaining acceptance among denominations. This final paradigm shift will usher in a new global expression of the church once believers realize the evangelical model of the last seventy years is insufficient to maintain the level of governance needed to fulfill God's will. My primary concern with the apostolic church is the problem posed by the sin of mental assent

---

[101] 1 Corinthians 13:9–13: "For we know in part, and we prophesy in part. *But when that which is perfect is come, then that which is in part shall be done away.* When I was a child, I spoke as a child, I understood as a child, I thought as a child: but when I became a man, I put away childish things. For now we see through a glass, darkly; but then face to face: now I know in part; but then shall I know even as also I am known. And now abideth faith, hope, charity, these three; but the greatest of these is charity" (emphasis added).

[102] Ephesians 3:9–11: "And to make all men see what is the fellowship of the mystery, which from the beginning of the world hath been hid in God, who created all things by Jesus Christ: *To the intent that now to the principalities and powers in heavenly places might be known by the church the manifold wisdom of God,* According to the eternal purpose which he purposed in Christ Jesus our Lord" (emphasis added).

(ever learning but never coming to the knowledge of operating in what we've learned). The church has attained much knowledge, understanding, and wisdom but has lacked in implementation, which is why sonship and kingliness is so important. To be a true son is also to be a progenitor of Him who sends us. It is not enough to be a child of God; instead, like Jesus, we must represent Him authentically. The new standard of church discipleship must come with the added development of operational spiritual dynamics in the believer with a dominion mind-set. The gifts and configurations of grace Jesus said we would have[103] must be developed to the fullness of the measure of Christ, which is given to each one as the Holy Spirit sees fit. This is where spiritual fathering benefits the most.

It wasn't until I found a mature man of God who was able to instruct me in the ways of God that not only did my personal growth accelerate but also many of my former religious positions were stripped away as I learned to die to self so that the Son of God could be revealed through me.[104] Becoming a disciple and submitting to a spiritual mentor has great benefits and is something that must be emphasized among all the churches there. Otherwise you may have crowd-following religious people building their own kingdoms. Within the church this is the weakness of the evangelical model; it is more heavenly minded than dominion

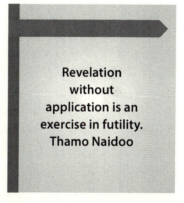

Revelation without application is an exercise in futility.
Thamo Naidoo

---

[103] John 14:10–12: "Believest thou not that I am in the Father, and the Father in me? the words that I speak to you I speak not of myself: but the Father that dwelleth in me, he doeth the works. Believe me that I am in the Father, and the Father in me: or else believe me for the very works' sake. Verily, verily, I say to you, He that believeth on me, the works that I do shall he do also; and greater works than these shall he do; because I go to my Father."

[104] Galatians 1:15–16: "But when it pleased God, who separated me from my mother's womb, and called me by his grace, To reveal his Son in me, that I might preach him among the heathen."

minded. The truth is that you must win on both fronts or else you lose both fronts and therefore live in perpetual postponement until another generation comes along that understands and can implement a compliant church paradigm. King David understood this and was able to win both battles. Because of this, he won both the hearts of the people and the territory assigned to them. God's enemies were defeated, and the land went into a period of rest.[105]

In the United States, our current president understands this but is fighting an internal battle within the ranks of the Republican Party, so their house is divided, giving the adversary an advantage as the forces that work against our freedoms are in favor of the globalization movement. Therefore, the Democrats continue to deceive the people, opposing everything that is good and just for our country. Should this administration not take on this responsibility and prosecute those who practice the lawlessness so prevalent in our government and win the battle over territory, it will eventually fail, and another cycle of renewal will need to be facilitated in the following generation just as it was in the book of Judges, where God's people went through thirteen repetitive cycles because, in spite of God's provision, they continued to fall away from His purposes. I am greatly encouraged by your new prime minister Imran Khan as he appears to stand with the people, against government corruption, and for the well-being of the people. I believe we're in a period where, because of the removal of the one who restrains and the rise of global nationalism, the Lord is intervening in the affairs of mankind and is calling His people to take a kinglier mantle and not just a priestly expression.

---

[105] 1 Chronicles 22:17–19: "David also commanded all the princes of Israel to help Solomon his son, saying, Is not the Lord your God with you? and hath he not given you rest on every side? for he hath given the inhabitants of the land into mine hand; and the land is subdued before the Lord, and before his people. Now set your heart and your soul to seek the Lord your God; arise therefore, and build ye the sanctuary of the Lord God, to bring the ark of the covenant of the Lord, and the holy vessels of God, into the house that is to be built to the name of the Lord."

Kings and Priests

One of the measurable changes we must see within the body of Christ is a shift from a priestly mentality to a kingly mentality. For centuries we have exceled in being heavenly minded (that's what it means to be priestly). We have aspired to excel in evangelism, worship, and service but have been weak in the dominion aspects of our mandate to be kings[106] (note the scripture says "kings" first, then "priests"). It is a Levitical posture to be priestly. The Levites (which means "to be attached") were never given a portion of the Promised Land because they had no desire for land. Their portion was to be attached to God; therefore, they dwelt among their brethren and served them. The problem with this is that God requires us to possess our inheritance. He needs someone to have a dominion attitude; otherwise, our adversaries control the territory. If you are priestly as a local body of believers, you will remain introverted and internalize your activity, having little impact in your community. This is why in the near future you will see a new paradigm begin to reveal itself as the manifestation of the sons of God is primarily the revelation of a mature church that will usher in the redemption of all things.[107] This is also the error of the consumer Christian, seeker-friendly church model and one of the last vestiges of the entrenched strongholds of the adversary. It internalizes a church into programs and activities that are self-serving and teaches that God is here to serve us and meet

Your paradigm determines your liturgy.
Thamo Naidoo

---

[106] Revelation 5:10: "And hast made us to our God kings and priests: and we shall reign on the earth."

[107] Romans 8:19–21: "For the earnest expectation of the creature waiteth for the manifestation of the sons of God. For the creature was made subject to vanity, not willingly, but by reason of him who hath subjected the same in hope, Because the creature itself also shall be delivered from the bondage of corruption into the glorious liberty of the children of God."

our needs with little emphasis on discipleship and equipping believers to achieve maturity. The signs of a seeker-friendly church are a lack of accountability for its members, performance-based worship, little or no teaching or discipleship, multiple programs for children but almost nothing for adults, no regard for the sanctuary or any sense of holiness in the assembly, and a constant revolving door of people cycling through it. Once spiritually hungry people see there's no depth, they will leave as the leading of the Holy Spirit draws them toward more compliant church models like the apostolic prophetic church model. The emerging apostolic, prophetic church paradigm will be the one that will usher in the unity of the church in this, the last season of God.

However, when we learn to become kingly (dominion minded), we will be like Him and start demonstrating justice and mercy toward those who like the adulterous woman (i.e., those who have sex outside of biblical marriage) in John 8:3–12, whom Jesus forgave and admonished to sin no more. Churches today have not sought the kingdom of God and its righteousness but rather have opted to embrace ungodliness in order to stay relevant in the eyes of society. We are in much graver danger of God judging us first. Therefore, let us humble ourselves, pray that God might heal our land, and cease prophesying judgment out of our own fleshy convictions. If the world hates God because of what they see in us, then we are neither His children nor His sons. But when we learn how to love the way God loves, even the fallen angels will know the wisdom of God and that He was right when He chose us over them.[108]

As continuing global unrest grows in the nations, now is the time for the church to rise to its potential during these latter days.

---

[108] Ephesians 3:9–12: "And to make all men see what is the fellowship of the mystery, which from the beginning of the world hath been hid in God, who created all things by Jesus Christ: **To the intent that now to the principalities and powers in heavenly places might be known by the church the manifold wisdom of God,** According to the eternal purpose which he purposed in Christ Jesus our Lord: In whom we have boldness and access with confidence by the faith of him" (emphasis added).

I pray that all those who claim to be followers of Jesus Christ seek God wholeheartedly and find the destiny God has for them. I pray you find some wisdom in these letters that will benefit you and those you labor with.

Lastly, take comfort in the words found in Psalms 2, that in spite of the global unrest, the church's best days are right in front of us. In the months and years ahead, the apparent warfare will be nothing more than the enemy's death throes as our adversary struggles with the reality that his time is near.

> Why do the heathen rage, and the people imagine a vain thing? The kings of the earth set themselves, and the rulers take counsel together, against the Lord, and against his anointed, saying, Let us break their bands asunder, and cast away their cords from us. He that sitteth in the heavens shall laugh: the Lord shall have them in derision. Then shall he speak unto them in his wrath and vex them in his sore displeasure. Yet have I set my king upon my holy hill of Zion. I will declare the decree: the Lord hath said unto me, Thou art my Son; this day have I begotten thee. Ask of me, and I shall give thee the heathen for thine inheritance, and the uttermost parts of the earth for thy possession. Thou shalt break them with a rod of iron; thou shalt dash them in pieces like a potter's vessel. Be wise now therefore, O ye kings: be instructed, ye judges of the earth. Serve the Lord with fear and rejoice with trembling. Kiss the Son, lest he be angry, and ye perish from the way, when his wrath is kindled but a little. Blessed are all they that put their trust in him.
> Psalms 2:1–12 (KJV)

Remember when I was with you how the Lord spoke of you being a gateway church? You have the capacity to be a doorway through which many will come and serve God in Pakistan, so take seriously the responsibility to develop a church model that can sustain a large number of meetings and host the purposes of God. The churches in Durban excel in this and are a good example for you to model your ministry after, being gateway churches themselves. Remember that the heart of God toward the sons of Ismael (Muslims) is full of love and healing. Seldom have I experienced warmth and generosity like I did among the people of Pakistan in Lahore. And as the message of the gospel spreads, I expect to hear great things from you.

Greet your family and the pastors for me.

Blessings. Madson

To the Believers in the United States

AS WE PROGRESS THROUGH this period of God's timeline, we find ourselves with the realization that God's desire was to establish the United States as a city set upon on a hill. We have from the time of our founding been the recipients of an undeserved portion of the grace of God (grace as in a supernatural deposit that empowers you to fulfill God's will for the purpose, He has called you to). As nations have developed since the turn of the last century, the United States has been an example of a nation-state in the similitude of the future kingdom, a kingdom within a kingdom, a theonomous people in an autonomous culture. If we are to continue on this course, we are in desperate need of a spiritual renewal that will unite us a people of purpose. This renewal will not be like the revivals of past generations but will reflect a maturing church. The revivals of the past were times of refreshment but ultimately produced little in the way of lasting societal impact.

We will continue to see the dismantling of the globalist movement as the gates of hell will not withstand the advancement of the kingdom of God as the church moves in the love of God, empowered in a way that previous generations believed in but never saw. For this to happen, the church will have to make a major shift away from its evangelistic paradigm and toward a more relevant expression of the fullness of God's plan. Ultimately the removal of restraint means God's expectation of His people globally has increased and we are no longer free to represent Him as merely His children. Instead we must exercise the maturity of His sons and daughters in the example of the person of Jesus Christ, the pattern Son. The priestly attitude of past generations caused the church to disconnect from its earthly responsibilities. The lack of political involvement by the church created a vacuum that was filled by the ungodly. The infiltration of our educational system by the postmodernist left could take years to undo as the regressive policies of the globalist movement have all but destroyed the foundations of our country through our education system. All the while the church stood idly by, abstaining from the involvement required to protect our sovereignty because it preferred to trust in an escapist mentality rather than take responsibility to secure the church's position by engaging ourselves. Because we are a free people and have the power of choice, we must also realize that the consequences of those choices have brought us to this place of irrelevance in the grand scheme of things as our adversary has for the most part neutralized the church in the USA and severely hindered God's work across the globe. It's time to engage and become the driving force for the good news of the gospel among the nations once again.

The three previous administrations of our country have fallen victim to the influence of principalities, powers, and rulers of darkness of the spirit of this age. It does not surprise me that these powers would unleash a torrent of adversity against anyone who would challenge conventional wisdom and the agenda of our adversary and the darkness that comes with it. Christians represent about 80 percent of the population of the United States but make up only about half the eligible voting populace who actually votes in the national elections—even less in local and state elections. If the church would simply engage and vote its conscience, then Judeo-Christian values would once again be the preeminent values of our country. Vote against bigger government, against wasteful spending, and against the proliferation of ungodliness. Vote for life and the protection of the unborn. Vote out the liberalism and leftist postmodern representation that is set on changing the course of our country and the loss of our freedoms bringing us under the control of an adversary who only wants to steal, kill, and destroy everything that is good and of God.

A Tree Is Known by Its Fruit

As leadership goes, we often look to the character of those who are seemingly confident and appear to be of good character, but their outward appearance often disguises their inward weaknesses. King Saul was a man who looked the part, but because he never understood his role, he ruled poorly and eventually lost his kingdom to David. He did not receive the Godly counsel of Samuel, and it cost him not only his sanity but also his life and the lives of his sons. David learned to be king by both accepting instruction and also learning from the errors of King Saul's mistakes. He served King Saul before he received the mantle to rule even though he had been ordained fifteen years earlier as king. Nevertheless, David was not a man of perfect character. He had had an affair and not only killed Bathsheba's husband but also about three dozen others in the process. He had fought both the lion and the bear and had won, yet his personal life and family were less than perfect. He died in grief over his son Absalom, but still God called him a man after his own heart because he maintained a shepherd's attitude toward the people all the days of his life. Before him there were many who failed and did terrible things, but God used them anyway, and they are remembered for their faith and good works and not their character. Isn't that like God to redeem the worst of us in spite of ourselves?

Therefore, let us be careful about whom we judge, whether they are fit for the job or not, but rather let us examine the fruit of their works to see if those works bear witness that they are being used of God to the furtherance of His kingdom. Let us look to see if they do good according to the scriptures and not do bad according to the cunning craftiness of men to keep us in bondage like the previous US administration did. I was sorely disappointed in our last president Barack Obama; he had an outward charismatic and appealing appearance, but a divisive agenda, moving the US towards ungodliness and towards the globalist agenda. Had Hillary Clinton been his successor we would have most certainly fallen under a Jezebel spirit and the damage may have been irreversible in the short term. As the battle for the soul of the United States continues, I believe our adversary will advance the Democratic party nomination for president of a woman to fulfill the goals they sought to accomplish through Hillary Clinton, because our adversary needs a Jezebel spirit to complete the emasculation of men and keep them suppressed to complete his plan to subjugate the United States into the globalist mandate. This defies Gods divine protocol of the patriarchal system and holding men responsible for the well-being of women, orphans and widows. Don't misunderstand me I have nothing against women is leadership, if fact I encourage it. But everything should be done in order and follow God's divine protocol. However, if at this time should the church fail to engage in the political process it will continue to lose its identity in society as its passivity continues to create voids in the public arena that the ungodly continue to fill. Should we continue down this path we will lose the Judeo-Christian foundations that developed our culture and the prosperity that we have enjoyed. And the good we have accomplished as a nation throughout the earth could be lost.

My purpose in writing this book is mainly because at a time when the world is engaging in unprecedented global cultural sifts the church is once again silent when it should be heralding Gods truths. Have we abandoned our responsibilities to speak on Gods behalf in the public arena at the national level? And to also bring the multifaceted expressions of the church to a commonality of core beliefs that unite us as a people in the unity of our faith and to challenge those among us who have been deceived by the enemy and have strayed from God plan for their lives and are no longer being transformed into the image of Jesus Christ the pattern son, to return to their pursuit of God no longer living in fear and subjugating ourselves to those things that are of the kingdoms of this world. Perhaps it's time we put aside our differences, and stop hating. We can continue to battle in the flesh or take the battle where it belongs and focus our attention towards, the principalities, powers, rulers of darkness and spiritual wickedness in high places.

We have yet to see the fullness of what God has planned for us, but let us be challenged to engage and do our part as the body of Christ in our generation lest we stand before God one day and be rebuked of our mediocre expression of our faith and our anemic disposition in the light of what Jesus did for us. Jesus suffered and died to gain our redemption and make a way to restore us to fellowship with God, not only as His children but also His sons. Yet He raised himself from death to show us we too could overcome if we would only follow after Him, authentically.

As I travel around the world teaching and training the next generation of leaders, my heart has always been for the US church, but God has in His wisdom sent me to some of the most destitute and unsafe places on the planet instead. The compassion that God has for the lost and suffering is overwhelming. He is full of love, kindness, and mercy for those who are hurting, but He needs His people to stand in the gap and become the conduit by which He can work through.

I hope these letters and teachings have added to your understanding and have some value for your personal growth and well-being. I pray the God of peace finds you well, that your needs are being met, that the Holy Spirit finds a place of sensitivity in your heart so that you may be in constant communion with Him, that the life of Christ emanates from you because you know Him, and that His light shows through in every aspect of your expression of the life He's called you to.

Blessings. Madson

About the Author

IN 1994, AT THE age of thirty-five, I had a personal encounter with the living God, my own Damascus road experience, a spiritual rebirth if you will. This transformed my life and started me on a path that would take me into a season of great trials and suffering, but it was also a path of purpose and consecration. This journey gave me new insight and the understanding that only comes through an experiential walk with our heavenly Father. It eventually led me to attend Bible college, start my own business, and develop a successful ministry as an itinerant lecturer, teacher and conference speaker. I learned what it meant to become a true disciple and eventually to use the grace and spiritual gifts He gave me as a catalyst that would take me into a deeper relationship with Him. May the words written here be an encouragement to you as you find God's truth in your own journey with Him.

Located in the heart of America "G.A.T.E. Ministry Fellowship" (Grapevine Apostolic Transformation Enterprise) is based in Kansas City USA. GATE'S mission is to build relationships in ministry by providing resources for churches desiring to transition into a higher level of expression and authenticity in both their local church and mission outreaches.

For more information about the ministry of Madson Baptiste go to: madsonbaptiste.com